ABSEGAMI YESTERYEAR

"Happy Birthday"
"Skip" 8/4/64
from
Mom & Dad

STATE OF NEW JERSEY
OFFICE OF THE GOVERNOR
TRENTON

RICHARD J. HUGHES
GOVERNOR

The harvest from New Jersey's Tercentenary celebration in 1964 promises to be rich.

New books, new plans, new interest in the story of the State's three centuries of people, purpose and progress, a new sense of community that may lead us to an understanding of ourselves and our world: these are the fruits that should come from this first statewide celebration in our history.

ABSEGAMI YESTERYEAR is a significant contribution to the story of New Jersey as it recounts the colorful history of Atlantic County, deep in the pines of South Jersey. Through this publication, we know of another aspect of Atlantic County, its rich historical heritage, that lies within the reach of every visitor to the more familiar New Jersey shore.

Jack Boucher and the Atlantic County Historical Society are to be commended for giving us ABSEGAMI YESTER-YEAR.

May, 1963

RICHARD J. HUGHES
GOVERNOR

NEW JERSEY TERCENTENARY
1664 · 1964

ABSEGAMI YESTERYEAR

By

JACK E. BOUCHER

Photography by the Author

A PRESENTATION BY

The Atlantic County Historical Society

Published by

THE ATLANTIC COUNTY HISTORICAL SOCIETY

Library of Congress Catalog No. 63-17029

First Printing—October 1963

Second Printing—November 1963

Printed in the United States of America

LAUREATE PRESS, INC., EGG HARBOR CITY, NEW JERSEY

Table of Contents

Introduction

We in Atlantic County, as in all other counties in the State of New Jersey, enjoy reaching back into the past, to speak of the building of ships or the manufacture of iron from bog ore, or the making of glass or salt. Our reflections dwell upon stagecoaches, Indians, and the armies of the Revolution, and upon Jersey's many contributions to America.

We speak of our historical heritage with pride, and yet it has become quite remote to many of us because time has taken its toll of our historic areas. Fire, weather, vandalism, and "progress" are among the agents of destruction.

Absegami Yesteryear has captured, in picture and word, vanishing Americana in historic Atlantic County. Through its pages, the reader may reminisce, he may grasp an appreciation of what lies in his backyard. And the reader has a pictorial "do-it-yourself" historical tour guide for trips to these significant areas. The handsome historical map and magnificent photographs with meticulously researched descriptions should prove an invaluable tool for the historian, amateur or professional.

Those of us who will read of these historic sites, then search them out, will be able to grasp the vital part they played in the growth and development of Atlantic County and New Jersey . . . particularly in our fight for independence from England when every ounce of resources was needed.

To some this may be just another book that "we should have" but that we never read because we are attracted to the more brightly colored, more strongly accented books that focus on the present. Should you belong to this group, my advice would be to just gently replace this book on the store shelf and walk out.

If, on the other hand, you feel that you are harboring thoughts about the distant past and yet you are not sure why, perhaps this book will clarify your thoughts and join together the pieces, past and present. There are some people who believe their ancestors are still present in spirit, and in themselves, too. Perhaps you won't admit it, but haven't you, while visiting a completely unfamiliar place, experienced the feeling, "I've been here before, but when?"

Seeing the many places shown and described in *Absegami Yesteryear* could result in such an experience.

The Atlantic County Historical Society is pleased to acknowledge the generosity of Jack E. Boucher for his many fine photographs and his hours of labor in writing, laying out, and co-ordinating all of the details of this book. Our appreciation to him and to our Historian, Mrs. Leonard G. Rundstrom, who, through many hours of careful research, has verified the historical facts appearing in this book.

The Atlantic County Historical Society is proud to present *Absegami Yesteryear* to you and to the future, and to dedicate this work to New Jersey's Tercentenary Year, 1964.

Mark D. Ewing, President
Atlantic County Historical Society

7

Special Acknowledgments

to

EDWARD F. MERRIGAN

Linwood, New Jersey

. . . whose constant assistance and companionship during the two years this work was in preparation meant so much to the success of our photographic forays, the results of which appear here. . . .

MRS. LEONARD G. RUNDSTROM

Absecon, New Jersey

. . . for her tireless research into our historic past, which has produced much of the information and fresh fact recorded here. . . .

and

RAYMOND N. BAKER

Pleasant Mills, New Jersey

. . . whose superb pencil sketches of early South Jersey in the chapter titles recall a portion of our heritage no longer available to the lens. . . .

My grateful appreciation . . .

JACK E. BOUCHER

June 1963

Foreword

The rich historical heritage of South Jersey, and especially of Atlantic County, has long been slighted in the world of books and publications. Even those who live in this significant region have failed to appreciate what lies at their doorstep. And only occasional newspaper articles have reminded us that Atlantic County served nobly in shaping the face of America.

Absegami Yesteryear will help to fill this gap by making Jerseymen, as well as readers elsewhere, conscious of the part these coastal pine barrens have played in our history. It is presented in narrative form, supplemented by the copious use of interpretive photography. And though our history is told in story style, the text is a factual one.

We claim nothing that research cannot prove. The publishings of earlier writers have been used as sources, but every effort has been made to authenticate facts. If errors occur, we hope readers will inform us, so that we may correct them in a subsequent edition. Errors have a way of perpetuating themselves because knowledgeable individuals hesitate to be constructively critical.

Many of the historic sites of Atlantic County, like scores of others around America and the world, are disappearing because of the inroads of modern civilization. The pitiful condition of many of our local treasures is reflected in the photographs.

Organizations dedicated to the preservation of antiquities, such as the National Trust for Historic Preservation, the Society of Architectural Historians, the National Park Service, the New Jersey Historical Society, the Atlantic County Historical Society, and others, can accomplish only so much. These organizations must rely on the co-operation of individuals like the reader of *Absegami Yesteryear* for encouragement and support. For only through a unified effort on the part of all Americans can the historical treasures of America—and New Jersey—be saved for future generations.

If you are encouraged because of this work to lend your support, in any form, or to visit these areas, or if you have become conscious of the hitherto little known treasure trove of antiquities available in Atlantic County, then the effort expended in this presentation has been worthwhile.

We hope this book will prove useful, entertaining, and inspirational to the serious historian and the amateur history buff, as well as to those who are strangers to our past.

Our special thanks for valuable assistance go to Charles F. Kier of Hammonton, New Jersey, and Thomas Matteo and Franklin Kemp of Atlantic City; the Pennsylvania Historical Society, for making available material regarding Richard Somers and stage routes in South Jersey; Robert Lunny, Executive Director of the New Jersey Historical Society, for use of the photograph of the Batsto Cypher; Mark Ewing, President of the Atlantic County Historical Society, and the Society membership, for undertaking the publication of this work, and Mrs. Sylvia Fried of New York City, our copy editor.

Thanks also go to Paul Burgess of Brigantine, for the loan of the 1722 deed to Somers Point, and to those members of the Atlantic County Historical Society who devoted much time to the distribution of publicity, the filling of advance orders, and the careful counter-checking of the text for errors. These members include Mr. and Mrs. Paul Cope, Mrs. G. Ruffin Stamps, Mrs. Mark D. Ewing, Mrs. Elmer Cunard, Miss Mida Blake and Miss Emily Smith.

J.E.B.

June, 1963

New Jersey's Historical Heritage

Three centuries of People, Progress, and Purpose, from 1664 to 1964, will be celebrated by the State of New Jersey during its Tercentenary Year.

Fourth of the original thirteen colonies, New Jersey has had a colorful history, which dates from aboriginal times. No one knows when the first Indian set foot on what one day would be the Garden State. Traces, however, have been found in South Jersey of an early civilization that existed six thousand years ago.

Henry Hudson, sailing aboard the *Half Moon,* sighted Cape May and recorded the event in the vessel's log in 1609, and early Dutch settlers a few years later marked two rivers bounding a twenty-mile-wide spit of land as the Great Egg Harbour River and the Little Egg Harbour River, which is now known as the Mullica River.

When the huge schools of whales declined along the New England coast in the mid-seventeenth-century, many fishermen of the area migrated to South Jersey, to Town Bank on the Delaware River, in Cape May County.

America's struggle for freedom in the War for Independence centered in the colonies from Virginia to Massachusetts, and New Jersey was in the midst of the fray. Washington's battles at Morristown, Princeton, and Trenton were high points of the Revolutionary War, and from these times to the middle of the nineteenth century, there took place a great period of growth for New Jersey, during which industry came to the State in the form of iron furnaces and forges, glassworks, salt hay gathering, fishing, and, indeed, recreation, in the budding shore resorts.

New Jersey was the first governmental unit to use the motto *E Pluribus Unum* on coins or currency, doing so on a penny in 1786. The Continental Congress did not adopt a formal currency until five years later, in 1791.

During the Civil War, New Jersey contributed its share by sending troops of the First New Jersey Battalion to fight in the war against slavery. In the century that followed, New Jersey's growth was the equal of any State's. Its network of sandy Indian tracks and stage roads was replaced by one of the finest paved highway systems in the world. The inventive genius of its citizens created the submarine, certain firearms, the phonograph, and the electric light bulb. Railroads checkerboarded the State, to give way in time to vast airports and jetports. The population soared to a count of nearly seven million. Today, its products—the products of its people—include steel, textiles, caterpillar tractors, electronics, plastics, and food for the world from the vast acreage of truck farms, which give New Jersey its nickname, the Garden State.

Celebrating its Tercentenary Year in 1964, New Jersey and its citizens will recall with pride its progress and development. An extensive program of marking historic sites, books and publications such as this one, radio and television programs, pageants and shows, lectures and movies—all will serve to remind the world that New Jersey honors its accomplishments of the past three hundred years, and looks forward with assurance to its future.

. . . And now, welcome to

ABSEGAMI YESTERYEAR

Richard Somers, USN, Master Commandant

The Somers Mansion is located at the Somers Point traffic circle at the junction of Shore Road, Ocean City Boulevard, and the Mays Landing Road. Directions to related points of interest may be obtained at the Mansion, a New Jersey Historic Site, open daily except Monday to the Public.

During Washington's first administration, the United States began paying an "annual tribute" to the Barbary pirates for the privilege of trading in the Mediterranean. Dissatisfied with the nearly two million dollars that had been paid, the Bashaw of Tripoli, in 1801, declared war on our nation. On August 3, 1804, Commodore Edward Preble's fleet of the new American Navy sealed off the harbor of Tripoli in a blockade that was to make the Mediterranean safe for vessels of all nations.

AN OMINOUS quiet existed in the heavy late-summer air. The waters of the Mediterranean shimmered in the light of the setting sun. A handful of vessels of the United States Navy—the *Argus,* the *Vixen,* the *Enterprise,* the *Siren,* the *Constitution,* the *Nautilus,* the *Intrepid,* and others, lay hove to, continuing a blockade of the harbor of Tripoli that had begun in earnest thirty-three days before, on the 3rd of August.

Aboard the ships of the line, commanded by Commodore Edward Preble, were a group of young officers—all in their early twenties—whose names, along with Preble's, would one day be inscribed in the annals of American naval history: Decatur, Stewart, Wadsworth, Hull, and Somers. Richard Somers, of Somers Point, New Jersey, had recently been commissioned a Master Commandant, and was now commanding the *Nautilus.*

Five hard-hitting attacks and the blockade had produced a telling effect on the Bashaw of Tripoli. His fighting ships were unable to leave the harbor and were almost fish out of water. Intelligence revealed his arms and ammunition were nearly exhausted. Commodore Preble felt one more strike would be the *coup de grace* to spell victory for the Navy and America. The plan was probably born aboard his *Constitution.*

Preble, Decatur, Wadsworth, Somers, and their brother officers gathered about a large table in the Captain's quarters. Oil lamps, recently lighted and swaying with the vessel's gentle rocking, illuminated the low-ceilinged room, and the huge beams, wooden knees, and stanchions cast shadows that only added to the intrigue and excitement. Overhead, the sound of the crew at work, creaking lines and tackle, could be detected. The sun, now a fiery ball in the West, burned red through the tall masts, maze of rigging, and furled sails. As the ship swung at anchor, the last rays of the sun streamed through the latticed windows of the fantail.

As daylight vanished, the officers rose and grasped hands. They were officers and they were firm friends. And the final touches had been put to a daring plan long in preparation.

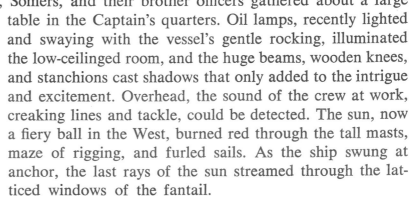

Master Commandant Richard Somers, as he appears in the only known painting of him

SOMERS MANSION
Somers Point, New Jersey

The ketch *Intrepid* had been the scene nearby of bustling activity. Seamen had been swarming about her, and light boats had been transporting a dangerous cargo to her hold and compartments. Planking had been secured in the broadest portion of the hold, and a hundred barrels of gunpowder, totaling some fifteen thousand pounds, had been emptied inside. The special compartment was just forward of her principal mast, and a train of powder was led aft to the cabin window, through a tube; another was led into the forepeak.

On the deck, around the mast, and directly above the magazine, was stacked a huge quantity of fused shells of many sizes, between one hundred and fifty and two hundred and fifty in number, ranging from nine to thirteen and a half inches.

The *Intrepid* was to sail her final voyage. She was to be a fire ship that would be sent into the harbor of Tripoli and there exploded amidst the Turkish vessels. Master Commandant Richard Somers, born just twenty-five years before in Somers Point, was to lead a minimum party of volunteers to perform the mission.

Two craft were to accompany the *Intrepid,* a four-oared boat from the *Siren,* and a six-oared cutter of the *Constitution* —thus doubling the chance of escape for Somers and his men once the fated *Intrepid's* powder fuse trains had been lit. Twelve men in all were selected for the mission, from among scores of volunteers.

At eight o'clock in the evening, the gallant men hoisted the *Intrepid's* anchor. Darkness covered their actions. The *Argus,* the *Vixen,* and the *Nautilus* spread canvas and followed the *Intrepid* a portion of the distance to the harbor entrance, then hove to.

A deed to the Somers Plantation of 3,000 acres to John Somers, dated 1722. This is Somers Point today. (Deed courtesy Paul Burgess)

The distance between the *Intrepid* and her sister ships increased until the fire ship and her crew were swallowed up in the inky blackness of the Mediterranean night. Every eye aboard the remaining three craft strained to follow their disappearing shipmates.

It was not long before the shore batteries of the Bashaw of Tripoli began firing. . . . The *Intrepid* had been detected. Bursts of flame spouted from the castlelike fortresses of the harbor.

Captain Stewart and a Lieutenant Carrol were standing on the deck of the *Siren*, long glasses to their eyes, trying to detect a glimpse of the fire ship, when Carrol shouted: "Look! See the light." A light was visible, passing and waving, as though a lantern were being carried by some person quickly along a ship's deck. Then it vanished.

". . . the whole firmament was lighted with a fiery glow, a burning mast, with its sails, was seen in the air, the whole harbor was momentarily illuminated, the awful explosion came, and a darkness like that of

Finger ring presented to Richard Somers by George Washington, containing a lock of the first President's hair

doom succeeded. The whole was over in less than a minute; the flame, the quaking of towers, the reeling of ships, and even the bursting of shells, of which most fell in the water, though some lodged on the rocks. The firing ceased, and from that instant, Tripoli passed the night in a stillness as profound as that in which the victims of this frightful explosion have lain from that fatal hour to this." Thus reads a description of the action given by a descendant of Richard Somers, believed to have been obtained from an eyewitness.

Master Commandant Richard Somers and his men perished in the service of their country. It will never be known definitely why they were unable to escape . . . if they fired their ketch on schedule . . . if an accident fired it early . . . or if a shell from a shore battery found its mark.

Since the explosion did not cause the anticipated damage to the harbor, it is even possible that Somers and his men faced capture in the two hours they were out of sight, and deliberately fired the craft and sealed their own doom rather than have the munitions on the fire ship fall into the hands of the enemy.

Thus did Somers and his men help set a pattern—even give birth to a tradition—among the fighting men of America's armed forces.

Certificate awarded by the Department of the Interior, National Park Service, under the Historic American Buildings Survey, to the Somers Mansion, for its unusual architectural and historical significance

·DEPARTMENT·OF·THE·INTERIOR·
·WASHINGTON·D·C·
·THIS·IS·TO·CERTIFY·THAT·THE·
·HISTORIC·BUILDING·
·KNOWN·AS·
The Somers Mansion
SOMERS POINT
·IN·THE·COUNTY·OF·
Atlantic
·AND·THE·STATE·OF·
New Jersey
·HAS·BEEN·SELECTED·BY·THE·
·ADVISORY·COMMITTEE·OF·THE·
·HISTORIC·AMERICAN·
·BUILDINGS·SURVEY·
·AS·POSSESSING·EXCEPTIONAL·
·HISTORIC·OR·ARCHITECTURAL·
·INTEREST·AND·AS·BEING·WORTHY·
·OF·MOST·CAREFUL·PRESERVATION·
·FOR·THE·BENEFIT·OF·FUTURE·
·GENERATIONS·AND·THAT·TO·THIS·
·END·A·RECORD·OF·ITS·PRESENT·
·APPEARANCE·AND·CONDITION·
·HAS·BEEN·MADE·AND·DEPOSITED·
·FOR·PERMANENT·REFERENCE·IN·THE·
·LIBRARY·OF·CONGRESS·

·ATTEST·

 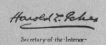

Seymour Williams
·District·Officer·

Harold L. Ickes
Secretary·of·the·Interior·

14   Antique furnishings on the second floor of the Somers Mansion museum

Restored cooking fireplace and implements

A monument to the Somers Family in a schoolyard on New York Avenue, Somers Point

Marker near Jobs Point on the Mays Landing Road, noting the Somers Ferry

NEAR THIS SITE AT
JOBS POINT WAS LOCATED
SOMERS' FERRY
ESTABLISHED IN 1693
TO CONNECT SOMERS POINT
AND BEESLEYS POINT

THIS MEMORIAL ERECTED
BY THE RICHARD BOWEN DIVISION
SONS AND DAUGHTERS OF THE PILGRIMS
JUNE 13, 1942

Shortly after the Battle of Tripoli, Congress passed a resolution honoring Somers and his comrades. A tall monument stands today on the grounds of the United States Naval Academy at Annapolis commemorating the battle and honoring Somers and his fellow officers. There have been six naval ships to bear the name *Somers* since 1812, the present being the destroyer U.S.S. *Somers*, DD947. And there is Somers Point, family homestead of the Somers' since before 1693.

IT WAS GLOUCESTER COUNTY then, in the waning years of the seventeenth century, when John Somers, born in England about 1640, settled on a spit of land bordering on the Great Egg Harbor River. Henry Hudson, aboard the *Half Moon* during his famed voyage along the coast, had discovered the river and called it Eyren Haven earlier in the century, on September 1 and 2, 1609.

Indians, a few hundred settlers — mostly fishermen — and mosquitoes were all that populated the region when Somers arrived on horseback. The solitary road to the region was but a rutted sandy path following for the most part an Indian trail. Midway between the Little Egg Harbor and Great Egg Harbor rivers it linked with a coastal trail. Travel through the Jersey pinelands had its dangers then, for the woods were still the home of panther, bear, and wolves.

Somers' wife and child had died during the crossing to the New World, but during a brief residence in Upper Dublin, Pennsylvania, he had remarried, one Hannah Hodgkins, an English Quakeress. Together, they finally settled on three thousand acres of land, the "spit" mentioned earlier. One day this would be called Somers Point; they called it then "Somerset Plantation."

At the meeting of the first court held at Portsmouth, Cape May County, later called Town Bank, John Somers was appointed Supervisor of Roads and Constable for Great Egg Harbor. It was March 20, 1693.

Crossing the swift waters of the Great Egg Harbor River was a hazardous undertaking except at the ebb or turn of the tide, and so it was that in 1693 John Somers, partly in his role as Roads Supervisor, and with the authority of the Provincial Congress, established a ferry "at the said Great Egg Harbor, which Person or Persons appointed by them for the Purpose aforesaid, shall and may exact for the Passage of every single person, Twelve-pence, and for Horses and Cattle Twelve-pence per head, and for Sheep and Hogs four-pence per Head, and for all manner of Grain, two-pence per bushel."

During their life at Great Egg Harbor, John and Hannah Somers raised six sons and three daughters, one of whom was the first Richard of the Somers clan. And it was Richard who, two years after his father's death, "burnt the brick" and built the fine mansion house that stands to this day, 238 years later, on a slight hill overlooking the river and bay.

A Friends Meeting had been established early in the 1700's in Cape May County, and all the Somers were devout members of the Great Egg Harbor–Cape May monthly meeting. Many are the accounts of these Jersey pioneer people traveling to meetings held variously at the Widow Garrison's, on the Cape May side of the river, and at the home of the Somers'. The stories of their travels to meeting, the crossing of the Great Egg Harbor River by canoe, boat, ferry, and even by swimming, are a testimonial to the hardiness and devotion of these Jersey settlers.

The second Richard Somers came on the scene in the mid-eighteenth century. He settled about a mile from the family homestead, on the Shore Road, in time, and became a surveyor, a colonel of the militia during the Revolutionary War, and a Judge of the County Court. He was a member of the Provincial Congress in 1775, but may have been inactive. It was his son, the third Somers to bear the name Richard, that would cement the family name in American history.

The third Richard was born September 15, 1778, great-grandson of the original John Somers, during the height of the Revolutionary War. Young Richard was sent to Philadelphia and then to Burlington for schooling. And both cities being major ports of the day, it is little wonder he became interested in the sea, at an early age.

For Richard Somers, aged about fifteen, is believed to have signed aboard a "coaster," a coastwise schooner, as a hand and then as a mate, about 1794, with little premonition of adventure and fame, however posthumous, to follow.

Young Somers received his warrant as a midshipman in 1798, virtually at the inception of the present United States Navy, and made his first voyage aboard the *United States 44,* Commodore John Barry commanding, senior officer of the service. A rapid but well deserved rise through the ranks followed, leading to his distinguished action and heroic fate at Tripoli.

George Washington, General and later first President of the United States, recognized Somers early in the young Jerseyman's career, and evidently held him in great esteem. Washington presented Richard Somers with a finger ring, containing a lock of his hair. The ring, now in the possession of the Pennsylvania Historical Society, has one of three known locks of Washington's hair.

THE SOMERS FAMILY reached its climax with Master Commandant Richard, but many descendants survive today. This has been not only their story, but ours, New Jersey's and America's. For Richard Somers, a youth in a youthful country and navy, set a pattern in patriotism and devotion that Americans can follow, and have always followed. Richard Somers, of Somers Point, New Jersey.

Only this modest stone and bronze monument remains to mark the birthplace of Richard Somers.

Somers Family burying ground adjacent to Mays Landing Road

Restored Living Room on second floor of Somers Mansion

Indian Trail to Stage Coach

TWILIGHT WAS swiftly approaching, and the encampment on the sandy shore would soon be still. Campfires blazed before a half-dozen thatched-mat lean-tos and huts. Dense smoke billowed skyward from some, to envelop hanging strings of curing shellfish.

Yards away, on the shore of the bay, silhouetted figures were beaching crude dugouts and carrying ashore woven baskets heavily laden with the day's netted harvest of fish. The whining of mosquitoes and splashing of water were punctuated occasionally by terse comments from the laboring men.

Twilight was indeed at hand, not only for the day, but for an era, and for a race of people. The laboring figures were Indians, remnants of several tribes of the once magnificent nation of the Lenni Lenape. Scheyechbi had been their home for more moons than legend could recall, in their *Walum Olum,* but it was the early eighteenth century, and the white man was settling everywhere. Even the name of their land — Scheyechbi — was being changed. The intruders were calling it Nova Caesarea — New Jersey.

The Great Egg Harbor River and Bay region had been their favorite summering place. The waters abounded with fish and the tidal flats with shellfish; on the sandy beaches were more birds' eggs and berries than the Indians could carry. This aboriginal resort area provided the Lenni Lenape with enough food to last the cold winters.

Frost and chill winds marked the end of the encampments, and the harvest complete, the thin line of bronze figures would head for the pine timber, for the trail to Chickohacki, called by the white man, "Little Worth" or "Trenton" . . . or to Burlington. The footpath, deeply worn by these annual pilgrimages, wound along the shores of the river, cutting inland at Mays Landing, and through the trackless forests, past what would one day be Weymouth, Hammonton, Folsom, and thence linking by way of trails to villages in the protected highlands.

Both the Great Egg Harbor and the Little Egg Harbor rivers in this area appealed to the Lenape. Their campsites, as evidenced even today by the discovery of arrow and spear points, flint chips, clay pottery fragments, celts, and other artifacts, dotted the shorelines of the watercourses.

"Their houses or wig-wams were sometimes together in towns, but mostly moveable, and occasionally fixed near a spring or other water, according to the conveniences for hunting, fishing, basket making, or other business of that sort, and built with poles laid on forked sticks in the ground, with bark, flags, or bushes on the top and sides, with an opening to the south, their fire in the middle . . . at night they slept on the ground with their feet towards it . . . their clothing was a coarse blanket or skin thrown over the shoulder, which covered to the knee and a piece of the same tied round their legs, with part of a deer skin sewed round their feet for shoes. . . ."

In 1935 a dugout canoe was discovered in Galloway Township, along the south shore of Nacote Creek near Port Republic. Originally some fifteen feet long, the craft was three feet wide and nine inches deep. Despite its long interment, charring done in the hollowing and shaping of the canoe was still evident. Unfortunately, the invaluable remnant of the past was not turned over to a museum, or chemically treated to resist deterioration, and in a brief time crumbled to powder.

But the finding of the dugout marks Chestnut Neck as a prime Indian village site. Farther north, along the Mullica, Clarks Landing and Batsto were scenes of aboriginal activity. Other such areas in Atlantic County include Wigwam Creek, Smithville; Pleasantville; Somers Point; Stephen's Creek in Estellville; Catawba near Mays Landing; English Creek; Patcong Creek; Pennypot; Folsom; Innskip (Blue Hole); and four locations around what is today Hammonton. Of these, the Somers Point site is conceded to be the largest and most significant by archaeologists. Unfortunately, a golf course and dozens of homes cover the site, precluding

An advertisement appearing in Dunlap's Pennsylvania Packet for March 20, 1775.

any on-site investigation, and little may ever be learned of the settlement.

Trails linked all of these areas. A path paralleled the one mentioned earlier, but on the western side of the Great Egg Harbor River. Starting at Beesley's Point, it wound past Tuckahoe and Stephen's Creek, and continued inland. Invariably, these obscure paths would strike for the tiny streams that fed the major rivers, for it was to these that the herring would come to spawn in season, offering rich pickings for the food-seeking Lenape.

Jersey's Lenape Indians traveled always by foot, horses being unknown to them. Everything — food, furnishings, equipment — was carried by hand, on their backs, or atop their heads, although this latter means was not as common as it is in primitive countries today.

Certain bands of Indians would, by mutual consent and usage, consider definite areas their hunting and fishing grounds. These bands, seldom numbering more than one or two hundred Indians, included the Kechemeches in Cape May County, the Manahawkins in Burlington and Ocean Counties, and the Tuckahoes and Absegami in what is now Atlantic County. Their memory survives to this day in the place names of our area: Absecon and Absecon Island from the Absegami; Tuckahoe from the Tuckahoe band; Catawba; Batsto — the watering place; Nesco and Nescochegue; Lake Lenape.

The Lenni Lenape—the name means "original people"—were of the Algonquian linguistic stock, and in New Jersey were divided into three major tribes. Those who inhabited South Jersey were called the Unalachtigo, and their totem was the wild turkey. Their arrival in the Atlantic County area is believed to have occurred during the Middle and Late Woodland Period, shortly following the invention of the bow and arrow. This would have been the period from about 500 B.C. to the sixteenth century.

Today, all that remains of Atlantic County's primitive inhabitants are traces of their villages and shell piles. Their descendants are Westward, their villages are now housing developments, their foot trails are paved roads. The Lenape are but a legend.

Lenape Indians all but vanished from the Jersey scene when the white man be-

gan cutting stage roads and horse trails crisscross about the Province. His settlements at Elizabethtown, Trenton, Burlington, Leeds, and elsewhere demanded commerce—the trading of food, powder, mail, and other staples.

The huge trees that for centuries had sheltered the Indian, and the deer, the bear, and the panther gave way to roads and farms, and in one hundred years New Jersey was transformed from a forested wilderness to the colonial capital of America.

In many instances, the colonists' roads followed the old Indian trails — and many of our highways today still do! The Indian had to walk . . . his route was often the shortest and most easily traversed. It made sense to follow his tracks.

South Jersey's early roads were rugged, rutted, sandy routes that tired the traveler. They were treacherous in three ways: shifting sands and the beating of horses' hoofs created traps for the wheels of the stages and wagons; wildcat, bear, and panther roamed the forest until late in the eighteenth century and were a constant threat, as were the Tory refugees who terrorized the pinelands until they were finally controlled by the militia. Jersey stages were often held up in the best, but later, traditions of the American West.

Streams and rivers always had to be forded, or if sufficiently wide, sometimes boasted a hand-propelled ferry service, in coastal areas. Inland, though, a stream meant danger, especially after heavy rains, when they would be swollen, deep and swift.

It is said that at Quaker Bridge, on the northern edge of Atlantic County, several persons lost their lives over the years, finally causing members of the Society of Friends to construct a crude bridge over

An advertisement as it was published on September 3, 1778, in the Pennsylvania Packet.

the water-course of the Atsion River, thus giving the area its name.

Many types of stagecoaches plied these routes. Some were enclosed, but many were open affairs, with rough plank seats. Because the stages were poorly sprung, the hapless traveler was subjected to a lurching, bumpy ride, behind a team of two to six horses. And a stage, speeding sometimes as fast as ten miles an hour behind a team of pounding horses, invariably generated dense clouds of stifling dust, which settled on driver, riders and cargo.

Small wonder then, the inns and taverns of the day, spotted at nearly every crossroad, did a thriving business in ale and applejack. Weary travelers, involved in a stage ride from Leeds (Leeds Point near Smithville) to Cooper's Ferry (Camden), which would consume most of two very full days' travel, stopped at every opportunity to refresh themselves, either at streams with water, or at inns with grog.

The sole road into what is now Atlantic County in 1777, according to the early map of William Faden published in that year, passed through Trenton, Burdentown (Bordentown), and joined at a hamlet in Burlington County known as Monrose with the road from Bridlington (Burlington). This track continued through since-vanished villages, including Crip's Mill, to Leeds, known now as Leeds Point. It then followed the coastline to Cape May Point.

By 1795 a second road pushed southeast to the coast from Cooper's Ferry through Haddonfield, Taunton, Atsion,

to Bur's Mill, Crip's Mill, and thence to Tuckerton. The colonial map maker that produced this interesting map placed Batsto some twenty miles from its actual location, and in such a position that there can be little doubt that it is the road that continued through Batsto at one point.

Stage roads crisscrossed the county by 1834. An original map of that year, by one Thomas Gordon, reflects the rapidly developing southern end of old Gloucester County—three years later in February of 1837, the area would become all of what is now Atlantic County.

The road from Burlington and Mount Holly reached Atlantic County at Atsion, continued through Quaker Bridge, Batsto, Pleasant Mills, Gloucester (Egg

A section of the old stage road between Quaker Bridge and Batsto, it appears today much as it did then, in Yesteryear.

23

Harbor), skirted Wrangleboro (Port Republic), to Smithville and Leeds (Point). It joined there with a coastal road dating to the late seventeenth century, starting at Chestnut Neck, passing through Leeds and Smithville to Absecombe (Absecon), Doughty's (Pleasantville area), Bargaintown, and Somers Point.

A road branched from Bargaintown, cut west through the pines to Mays Landing, Weymouth, Pennypot, Blue Anchor, Williamstown, Long-A-Coming (Berlin), and on to Camden. Still another road headed north from Mays Landing to Batsto, crossing only one road and passing no towns between the two points.

A main stage road continued south from Mays Landing, through Stephen's Creek and Estellville, Tuckahoe, and on to Cape May. If it is difficult to imagine Atlantic County so sparsely populated, it is interesting to see that in 1840, the county had only about a dozen and a half villages with a total population of 8,726 people.

The stagecoach, wagon, and horse were the only means of transportation into Atlantic County as late as the first decade of the twentieth century—sixty years ago—other than the railroads, which pushed to the coast in the 1850's.

Even today, though the stages have vanished from their sandy routes and sleek strips of modern paving carry the traveler to his destination with a smooth, dust-free, effortless ride, there remain long reaches of woods roads that once served the public of long ago. They still remain, a bit of vanishing Americana, a monument to a bygone era in old Jersey, and an invitation to the explorer.

Stand in their midst, among the pines and cedars, listen to the wind in the treetops. Reflect on yesteryear . . . you'll see the stage driver high in his seat, cracking his whip over the team and shouting . . . and the stage, with its straining, sweating team spreading the dust your way. . . .

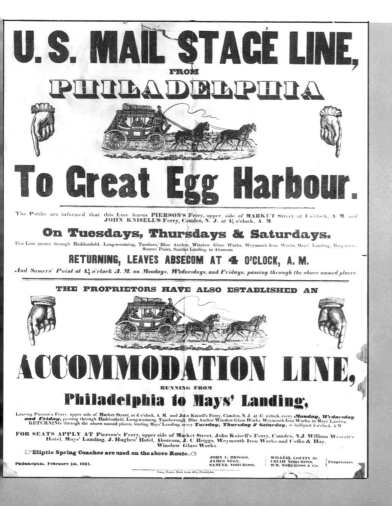

Poster advertisement, of 1841, hawking the mail stage from Philadelphia to Great Egg Harbor. The trip took two days.

24

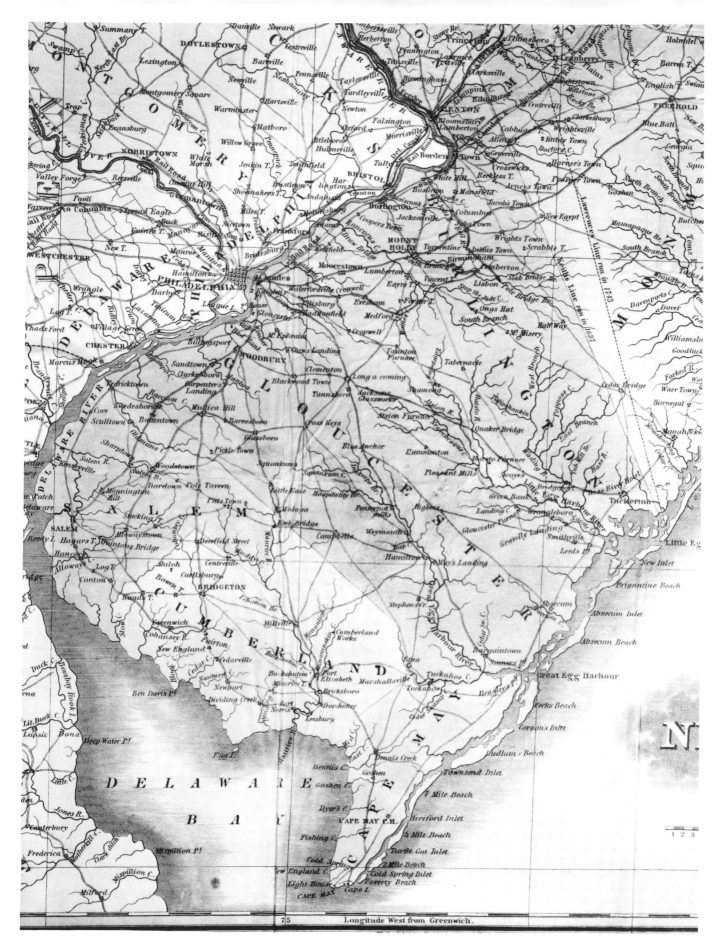

Map of South Jersey by Thomas Gordon, published in 1834, three years before Atlantic County was established, showing stage roads, villages, and the extent of old Gloucester County.

Inns and Taverns of Long Ago

WEATHERED CLAPBOARDS framed the windows of the old double-story inn, and warm yellow light filtered through the hand-blown wavy glass panes to mix with the fading rays of the setting sun. A late fall wind whistled through the big pines and cedars that cradled the long, narrow building.

Several horses stood quietly near the front door, tethered to a sagging log rail, and by the side of the inn a dozen chickens scratched about in the gravel of one of the paths that met to form a crossroads. In the distance could be heard the sound of hoofs and wagon wheels as a stage approached. . . .

The stage creaked to a weary halt. Its driver, bedecked in knee breeches, buckled shoes, and a weathered cap, clambered from his high seat to help a couple of passengers disembark. Trudging forward, he checked the harness and coach "tongue," patted one of the four huge horses, then swung back to the driver's seat. Its big ironclad wooden wheels biting into the rutted gravel road, the stage turned from the old inn and continued into the fading twilight to Leeds, terminus of the stage run.

The trip from Cooper's Ferry had not been unusually difficult, but it had been tiring. Seemed like the rough stage road boasted an extra rut with every trip, and fording the several streams along the route was never easy. And now with the arrival of winter. . .

Meanwhile, the passengers headed into the tavern, and with a long ride behind them in the unheated stage, they were eager to warm themselves before continuing to their respective homes.

The innkeeper greeted the arrivals at the door, holding it ajar while they entered tugging their bulky baggage. He glanced up at the sky, heavily overcast, and noted a few scattered flakes of an early snow drifting downward.

Candles illuminated the small, low-ceilinged room. Heavy-beaded beams, scarcely a foot above one's head, crossed the room, supporting the lodging floor above. Markings of an "up and down" pit saw lent a texture to the coarse joists. A roaring blaze burned in the huge fireplace, and the odor of burning oak permeated the room.

Only a couple of the tables were occupied, and flickering candles reflected in the eyes of the patrons as they gave the newcomers an appraising glance. No one traveled through old Gloucester County without receiving a once-over from the local gentry.

Across the wide pine-plank floor boards, was a counter — the bar. And a welcome sound indeed was the echo of pewter tankards being set firmly on its surface, ale spilling from their tops.

A blast of wind sent the door crashing open on the straining "HL" hinges, revealing an ever-increasing snowfall outside. The innkeeper turned to a lad of some ten years and shouted:

"Joby, fetch some fresh wood for the fire, we'll need it before the night is finished!" He then turned to carry the tankards of ale to the waiting customers, setting the brew on the rough-hewn tables.

Early taverns were the oasis for the traveler, and the nerve center for the community. Cold steins of ale or cider or glasses of Jersey applejack would refresh the weary wayfarer and better help him endure the lurching, bouncing stage rides along the dusty, narrow roads through the pines.

When the stage passed, the news arrived, and the village males would congregate at the inn to discuss the latest news from around the country, although by the time it arrived it could easily be up to a month or more late.

Occasionally, copies of the *Plain Dealer* from Bridgeton, the *New Jersey Gazette,* or the *Pennsylvania Packet* from Philadelphia would be delivered, and these would recount the affairs in Europe, the arrival and departure of sailing vessels in the port of Philadelphia, and the shipment of linens, china, and tea from England.

When the icy gales of winter swept the coast and snow covered the trails, the roaring fire at the inn would be a welcome sight. It must have been a warm, friendly atmosphere, bitter cold outside, a crackling fire in the hearth inside, with steaming kettles of soup or stew in the huge fireplace.

And the sleeping rooms upstairs! Tiny, narrow cubicles, barely large enough for a bed. With no heat other than a possible fireplace at the end of a hall, temperatures undoubtedly were as cold in the quarters as they were outdoors.

When, because of crowded stages or weather conditions, the inn was taxed beyond capacity, the innkeeper would assign several guests to the same room, and naturally the same bed. A stranger would not remain so for long in early South Jersey.

Whatever public life existed in the province found its expression in the tavern, and thus the innkeeper became a man of considerable influence. It was he who had the latest information on shipping and new arrivals at the ports; to him funneled announcements of births and deaths, of vendues and the sale of timberland. It was the innkeeper who knew of the latest doings of the legislature, the latest laws passed and repealed; he was the adviser on matters personal and legal; he would counsel the discouraged and praise the proud. The innkeeper was far more than a dispenser of spirits, his inn far more than a house. He was a friend in need, his house a haven. Nothing but the best would do for his guests, and for them he provided nourishment and knowledge.

Inns, taverns, and "ordinarys" were usually one and the same, since proprietors were required by law to maintain minimum sleeping quarters for guests if they served liquors. However, there were inns that were not taverns, such as the one maintained at the village of Leeds by one Japhet Leeds, late in the eighteenth century. Apparently, Leeds did not serve alcoholic beverages, keeping only a boarding house that offered food and lodging.

Here would be discussed the problems of the day, ranging from the quality of a day's hunting or fishing, crops and harvest, or a new child at the Steelmans, to the doings of the Army at Trenton or Morristown or the arrival of a privateer at Chestnut Neck.

Rates charged by the taverns and inns were fixed by the courts, and proprietors were required to display them according to law. An act, passed March 15, 1738, reads in part:

". . . and they and every of them ſo licenſed are hereby commanded and obliged, under the Penalty of Five Pounds, to be recovered and applied in Manner aforeſaid, to paſte on a Board, and hang up in View in the Moſt publick Room of his or her Houſe, the Liſt of Rates ſo delivered to him by the Clerk as aforeſaid, and that within forty-eight Hours after his Receipt of the ſame."

Some of these rates were as follows:

FOR MAN

Breakfast, common	25 Cts.		
ditto, extraordinary	31		
Dinner, Common	31		
ditto, extraordinary	50		
Supper, common	25		
ditto, extraordinary	31		
Lodging	12	1	2
Madeira Wine, per quart	$ 1	25	
Toddy ditto	25		
Cider, per quart	10		
Metheglin	31		
Best strong Beer, quart	12	1	2

FOR HORSE

Stabling, per night	20		
Oats, per quart	3		
Corn, per ditto	4		
Pasturage, per night	12	1	2

The inns and taverns of Atlantic County from colonial times to 1875 were legion. Most, including many well known hostelries, no longer exist, having vanished into the mists of yesteryear.

There was James Baremore's Inn at Smithville, which served the traveler from 1809 to 1813 at its location on West Morse's (Moss) Mill Road, adjoining a cemetery that still exists today. The spirits at Baremore's Inn were of a different variety than their "neighbors" next door.

Baremore was born in Philadelphia in 1765, coming to old Gloucester (Atlantic) County in 1790 to live in Galloway Township. He married one Eunice Leeds in the same year, and promptly proceeded to become active in business, including a real estate venture with one Peter Turner, in which the pair bought 881 acres of Brigantine Beach in 1802. A daughter, Hannah, married Isaac Smith, who in 1837 became the first High Sheriff of the new County of Atlantic.

Nearby was the Sign of the Spread Eagle, the two properties actually adjoining one another. It was operated by Jeremiah Bates from 1806 to 1813, and by Richard M. Risley from 1813 to sometime after 1814.

The Green Tree Tavern was situated on the "road from Blue Anchor to Leeds Point, at the intersection with a road from Absecon." It was opened in 1796 by one John Steelman, Sr. and operated by him until 1815, when the license was granted to Richard Higbee. A John Turner, of Galloway Township, purchased the tavern in 1829, and maintained the house until after 1833.

Payne's Tavern at Chestnut Neck was licensed in March of 1772, and was conducted by George Payne of Egg Harbor until it was burned by the British during the attack on this vital privateer's nest, October 6, 1778. Payne, called a mariner in early records of 1769, served in the Revolutionary War. He was commissioned a Captain, Third Battalion, Gloucester, in November of 1777, and First Major of the same battalion in March of 1778.

After the war, Payne was again granted a license to maintain a tavern, but the records do not reveal its location; the year was 1785.

Several miles west, along the headwaters of Nacote Creek at Clarks Mills, was Adrial Clark's Inn, licensed in 1793 and operated until 1805, and possibly later. Any trace of this old inn is lost until 1826, when one Alice Clark held forth here for two years. The next record shows Sherman Clark in possession until about the time of his death in 1849.

Clarks Mills eventually became Wrangleboro and Unionville. Today it is called Port Republic. The village contained in 1834, a *"store, one or more taverns, and one mill, and 15 or 20 dwellings,"* and was actually located about one mile west of the present center of Port Republic. It is marked today by the site of the Clarks Mills Meeting House and Revolutionary War cemetery.

There were two inns of note in Absecon (which was then spelled variously Absecombe, Abesekom, and other ways). One, the more noted of the pair, was Ann Risley's Tavern, at "Abesekom Bridge." This stopover was opened in 1763 by Peter Risley, in a building that had been his home from about 1736. Risley died about 1765, and his widow took out her license, holding it till a year before her death in 1786.

Her tavern was known far and wide for its generous hospitality. Records show that her menu included fish, crabs, clams, and oysters from nearby Egg Harbor Bay, as well as sugar, molasses, and rum from the West Indies.

The license application reads in part: "... the humble petition of Ann Risley, Widow of Great Egg Harbour Township, Gloucester County, in the Province of New Jersey, Humbley sheweth that your petitioner having kept tavern near Abesekom Bridge in the several years hath thought proper to acquaint your honours that she hath built her a house with stabling and other conveniences for the entertainment of travelers thereby doth humbly entreat your Honours to grant ... it being a suitable stage stop there being no other within ten miles. ..."

Licenses of the day were granted inn and tavern keepers only if their petitions were endorsed by individuals of good reputation. Among those signing for Ann Risley were Robert Morse (from whom Moss Mill Road took its name), John Somers, George Payne of Chestnut Neck, Richard Wescoat (whose name is spelled variously Westcott and Wescott), of The Forks, (Pleasant Mills), Micajah Smith, Sea Captain, and Timothy Shaler, noted Privateer Master.

John Holmes opened an inn at Absecon eleven years after Ann Risley closed her doors, his license being granted during the October term of court in 1796. This inn continued in business until after 1846, with only two noted changes of ownership. In 1814 one Hannah Holmes, his widow, assumed command until she married Israel Shillingsforth in 1817. Israel was then granted the license in 1818.

Across the salt marshes, on a spit of land that would become Atlantic City, Millicent Leeds, second wife of Jeremiah Leeds, the first white permanent settler on Absecon Island, opened an inn or boarding house in 1838, after the death of Jeremiah. This was located at the present corner of Baltic and Massachusettes avenues and was operated until about 1870.

Doughty's Inn of Great Egg Harbor Township, Gloucester County, another of the more important inns of the day, was located on the Old Delaware Road that "leads from Bargaintown to Thomas Doughty's Tavern." It operated from 1793 to after 1832.

Town meetings and religious services were held at Doughty's. One of the more noted Methodist circuit preachers of the era, the Reverend Richard Sneath, recorded in his diary in 1798 notes of his sermons at Doughty's, and religious services were conducted there for many years.

Somers Point boasted two principal inns, Abigail Somers' and Andrew Godfrey's. The Somers Inn was operated from 1826 to after 1827, and Godfrey's began in 1807 and operated until after 1816. The location of these two inns is indefinite.

At Pennypot, on the present Black Horse Pike where the Hospitality Branch of the Great Egg Harbor River crosses, was the Pennypot Tavern, called at one time the "Smashed Hat." A mill was located nearby. Isaac Dole was the tavern keeper here in 1763, and although it is not known when the subsequent owners took over or who they were, the inn did not cease to operate until after 1834.

An old diary written in August, 1843, contains the following entry: *"Every open space in the pines of New Jersey is a town. We passed en route Emmelsville, a place containing two taverns and three dwellings. . . . Pennypot or Smashed Hat is really a very funny name, but not more so than the appearance of the town . . . it is easy to conjecture how the latter originated. The hotel has never been known to average more than one pane of glass to each sash, the rest being substituted by pieces of boards and slabs, some of which had once been whitewashed, others were of a beautiful blueish grey. Storm Time & Co. were the painters. In two or three of the most conspicuous sashes were stuck something black, which the stage driver pronounced to be old hats, the whole giving to the hotel a singularly beautiful and variegated appearance."*

Mays Landing boasted two inns, including George May's, which opened in 1763, and Peter Wells's, which was licensed in 1778 and possibly before. No tavern licenses were granted during 1777 and 1778 during the occupation of Philadelphia by the British, leaving the dates of Wells's operation in doubt.

An advertisement in the *Pennsylvania Packet* of September 3, 1778, by Samuel Marryott states: *"a Stage Waggon will set out on Monday Morning from Peter Wells. . . ."* (See page 21.) Wells died in 1784.

The Sailor Boy Inn, located at the *"forks of Morse Mill, Absecon and Main Philadelphia roads,"* near the present village of Elwood, was owned in 1804 by one Joel Bodine, and continued in operation until after 1848.

The signboard of the inn was the figure of a sailor painted in blue, with a white cap and trimmings. Legend states the place obtained its name when a group of shipwrecked sailors making their way from the coast to Philadelphia with a quantity of salvaged rum in their possession stopped overnight in a clearing in the area and promptly proceeded to become "three sheets to the wind." Later, when Bodine opened his inn, the event with its alcoholic overtones suggested the name for the inn.

Owners of the Sailor Boy included Isaac and Rebecca Bolton, 1807; Rebecca Fowler, 1819; Arthur Wescoat, 1825; Absalom Steelman, 1826; John Turner, 1827 to 1834; Arthur Wescoat, Sr., 1834; Arthur Wescoat, Jr. and Absalom Steelman Wescoat, 1835; and William Bird in 1848.

Pleasant Mills, called in colonial times the "Forks," it being at the confluence of the Batsto and Atsion rivers, was the locale of four important taverns.

Richard Wescoat, First Major of the Militia during the Revolutionary War, and later called "Colonel," opened an inn at The Forks in 1764 and conducted business there until after the war; in 1783 he sold it to David Falkinburg.

The House of Richard Wescoat (Wescott) is believed to have been located in close proximity to the Mullica River, possibly an actual stone's throw from the stream, and less than one mile from Batsto, downstream. During the War for Independence, Wescoat's was a veritable beehive of activity, for it was here that most of the vessels seized as prizes by the privateers, as well as craft being traded by American owners, were unloaded and auctioned at public sale. Prospective buyers, or their representatives, came from Philadelphia and other distant points whenever a sale was advertised in the *Pennsylvania Packet* or the *New Jersey Gazette*.

An advertisement in the *Packet* on January 2, 1779, stated: *"On Monday, the third of January inst. at Col. Wescott's at the Forks of Little Egg Harbor,*

"The Schooner Fortune, with her tackle, apparel and furniture, per inventory. Also her CARGO, consisting of about three hundred barrels of flour, a quantity of Indian corn, and a valuable young Negro fellow.

"By order of the Court of Admiralty of New Jersey."

Another notice, published in the *New Jersey Gazette* of July 20, 1778 read: *"At publick vendue, at the house of Richard*

Wescott, Esq. at the Forks of Great-Egg-Harbor, on Tuesday the 28th day of July instant, between the hours of twelve and five, the following VESSELS, to wit, the brigantine Industry, sloop Dispatch, and sloop Molly's adventure: And on the day following, between the hours of ten and five, the sloop Canester, brigantine Carolina Packet, brigantine Prince Frederick, brigantine Speedwell, sloop Jenny, and the schooner Bachelor, with their respective tackle, apparel and furniture. . ."

Today, although Richard Wescoat's Inn and Tavern no longer exists, one may stand by the shore of the quiet waters of the Mullica, and with little effort visualize the courtyard of the tavern, bustling with activity, groups of men standing about discussing the sales of the day . . . newcomers riding up the dusty roads on horseback or arriving by stage . . . and the broad expanse of the Mullica crowded with brigantines, sloops, and other craft, their sailless masts and rigging tall among the pines, tugging at their anchor lines against the seaward-pushing current. It would have been an inspiring sight indeed, to anyone who followed the sea. . . .

Wescoat left the Forks in 1783 to open a hostelry at Mays Landing, only a

year after he was indicted for selling strong liquors without a license. His trial, brought before the Court of Common Pleas in June of 1782, resulted in acquittal.

The other important inns of the day at The Forks included the Lafayette Tavern, circa 1829 to 1837, owned by Nicholas Thompson; the Tavern of Benjamin Brush, dating from 1764 to 1784; and James Weeks's Inn, which operated from 1829 in *"the house where he now dwells on the stage road leading from Gloucester Furnace to Pleasant Mills."*

Such were the inns and taverns, now vanished, of a bygone era. They were places not only of entertainment, and rest and refreshment for the traveler, but public meeting places, for religious worship and village gatherings. Here were held the recruiting drives for the Continental Army and the Jersey Militia. They were voting places, and served also for public vendues —auctions. They were the focal point of community life, and have earned a deserved place in our history.

Of these places only a handful remain. They include the inns at Stephens Creek, Smithville, Port Republic, Nesco, Gravelly Run, Mays Landing, and Emmelville, and theirs is the story that follows.

An East Indiaman, trading vessel of the East India Company, and popular prey for privateers operating from the Forks. Many of these craft were sold under the hammer at Richard Wescott's Inn.

COURTESY: Book of Old Ships—
Culver & Grant—Garden City Pub.

31

The Franklin Inn*

*Located in Port Republic, on Mill Road, just north
of the Mill Pond dam, west side of the road.*

IT IS SAID William Franklin, son of Benjamin and Governor of New Jersey from 1762 to 1776 gave the Franklin Inn at Port Republic its name by virtue of occasional visits to the inn. The Tory Governor of the Colonial Province is known to have had a summer retreat along the Mullica River, probably at Lower Bank.

Franklin Inn, situated on the highest knoll along Nacote Creek is believed to have been built around 1750, and was located along a portion of the old stage road between Clarks Mills and Chestnut Neck, a branch of which continued through Smithville to the village of Leeds.

Nacote Creek during the eighteenth and much of the nineteenth century was one of the busy ports and shipbuilding centers along the South Jersey coast. Shipyards here serviced the privateers and coastal merchant sailers that plied the Atlantic seaboard. The vessels' crews and workmen alike found the hospitality at the inn welcome, after a day's toil or a voyage at sea.

While early records are vague, or nonexistent, it is definitely known that Micajah Smith, sea captain and privateer, had an interest in the place during the waning days of the eighteenth century and until 1807. Smith was one of the first to receive letters of marque and reprisal from the government during the Revolutionary War, and his own ship, the *Sly*, brought many fine prizes into Chestnut Neck.

Ownership of the inn was transferred in 1807 to Daniel and Phebe Mathis (Matthews) and they operated it for a period. The next recorded information shows one Jonas Miller in charge from about 1827 to 1835 or 1837. It was Miller who built a brick store adjacent to the inn about 1815. This brick store has been joined to the wooden inn building during reconstruction in recent years.

The Colwell family of Weymouth Furnace acquired the inn in 1835–37, and the brick store was used as a post office with James Hatfield as postmaster.

In time, the property was sold to General Elias Wright, and thence to the Ashley family of Port Republic, from whom Mrs. Harriet Sander, the present owner, purchased it, more than twenty-five years ago.

Today, the old Franklin Inn provides a picturesque scene. It is no longer an inn but a private residence. Although the tiny sleeping rooms have been removed to provide a more functional living room, much of the atmosphere of an old colonial inn remains, both inside and out.

And Port Republic, like the Franklin Inn, boasts a quiet charm, making it one of South Jersey's outstanding old country villages.

* Recorded in the Historic American Buildings Survey

Peter Steelman's, at Stephens Creek

Site at bend of private road of Atlantic County Game Preserve, east of Route 50 and four miles south along Route 50 from Route 40; Building has been removed to Smithville, New Jersey.

UNPAINTED weatherboards coarsened by the elements, its doors closed to the wayfarer, the old Peter Steelman Inn was located until recently along the stage road from Mays Landing, and points north and west, to Cape Island (Cape May).

Fires have not burned in the twin fireplaces at either end of the big room for decades, and the small, low-ceilinged rooms on the second floor no longer echo to the snores of weary men.

This was an inn that opened in 1811 and remained in business during the height of operation of the nearby Estellville Glass-works, until after 1836. The heavy-beaded beams of the tavern room are blackened with the smoke of years. Fine wood paneling surrounds the room, and much of the original hardware remains, including a crane in the brick-lined fireplace.

The archives show Peter Steelman applied to the Court of Common Pleas during the March Term in 1811, for a license to keep an inn *at the place where he lives in Stephens Creek, Weymouth township.* This license was renewed annually until after 1836.

The inn today is being reconstructed on the grounds of the Smithville Inn at Smithville, New Jersey.

Hiram Steelman, of Atlantic City, examines the grave marker of his ancestor, Peter Steelman, founder of the Stephens Creek Inn, who died in 1861, "aged 85 yrs 6 mos, & 6 days."

An iron pintle for window shutter and weatherboards ⟩

The weathered exterior of the Steelman Inn at Stephens Creek

Gone are the bar, the coarse tables and chairs, the sound of toasting and merrymaking. The inn is a ghost of itself, with unadorned wood paneling and a cold fireplace, and debris strewn about the floor.

Stage Stop at Gravelly Run

*Located on the Mays Landing–Somers Point Road, Route 559,
just 2.0 miles east of Mays Landing, on north side of road.*

A LICENSE *"to keep a Public House of Entertainment in the Place where he now lives"* was granted in June of 1770 to James Steelman of Gravelly Run, by the Court of Quarter Sessions of the County of Gloucester, the application being endorsed by such noted citizens of the era as Recompence Scull, Frederick Steelman, Joseph Ingersoll, Richard Somers, Elisha Smith, Nehemiah Leeds, Christopher Lucas, and Daniel Lake.

Thus it was that the Gravelly Run Tavern was opened to the public, to serve until well after 1834. Steelman, born in 1750, served in Captain Joseph Covenover's company during the Revolutionary War, and upon his return operated not only his inn but also a saw mill and possibly a grist mill nearby on the waters of Gravelly Run. Active in politics, he was Overseer of the Poor in 1798 and 1799.

Steelman's inn was, as were so many others, a public meeting house for civic affairs, and a record in a Road Return book for Gloucester County mentions for October 1810: *"The Surveyors of Highways for Egg Harbour, Galloway and Weymouth Townships are to meet at the House of James Steelman on November 1st, 1810. . . ."*

Ownership of the inn was turned over to William Treen, grandson of Captain William Treen, who with his vessels the *Unity* and the *Fame* performed outstanding services during the Revolutionary War. Captain Treen at one time was taken prisoner by the British and confined, ironically, aboard the prison ship *New Jersey*.

Grandson William, who married Rejoice Steelman was granted his license in 1827 and renewed it annually until 1832. By 1834 management was recorded under the name of George Treen, and

operation continued for an unknown period of time. By this time the inn was known as Treen's Tavern.

A sign, used in later years, has been preserved by the late Charles Abbott, who lived in his family's homestead across the road for three quarters of a century. This sign noted the building as the Gravelly Run Inn, and is dated 1811. Architectural features seem to indicate the existing building may not date before 1811, and it is possible a new structure was erected on the site of the original, or the original was merely extensively renovated early in the nineteenth century.

Weeds and vines today seek to claim the old structure, and the elements, entering through open doors, broken windows, and a rotting roof, are writing the final chapter to the story of the Stage Stop at Gravelly Run.

Remains of the brick fireplace among the debris of the crumbling Steelman-Treen Tavern at Gravelly Run

Samuel Snell's Tavern, later called Baker's Hotel, at Hamilton Bridge at Weymouth Road. Operated from 1765 to 1784 by Snell; from 1801 to 1815 by John Wheaton; by Jacob Adams from 1821 to 1836 and by James Baker before 1842. Snell served in both the army and colonial Navy during the Revolutionary War.

Old Emmelville Tavern, on Weymouth Road, 2.5 miles west of Mays Landing, on south side of road is now a private residence. The building dates from about 1800 and features architecture of the era, including wood-pegged mortise and tenon joints, split lath, and stone foundations.

Veal and Campbell Tavern at Buena Vista (formerly called Campbella). The earliest license authenticated for this tavern was granted to Enos Veal in March of 1814. Archibald Campbell was granted licenses during the years from 1816 to 1832. It is likely the tavern is far older, since the diary of Reverend Richard Sneath mentions in 1798, "preached at Archibald Campbells and Doughty's Taverns."

39

The Smithville Inn

Located on Route 9, the Shore Road, six miles north of Absecon, on the West side of the Road.

"*SMITHVILLE, village of Galloway t-ship, Gloucester co. 42 miles S.E. of Woodbury, and 2 miles E. from Leed's Point; contains a tavern, store, Methodist meeting house, and 10 or 12 dwellings, surrounded by pines and near the salt marsh.*" This is the description of the hamlet of Smithville by Thomas Gordon, in his gazetteer published in 1834.

Stages traveling the Philadelphia Road from Cooper's Ferry, via Long-A-Coming and Weymouth to Leeds Point, passed through Smithville, stopping there for passengers. Here were held the meetings of Galloway Township for many years. And here was the voting place for many an election of long ago.

Early records of the property are traced to 1737 and one John Smith. A Jesse Smith is known to have owned the property before 1800, but no positive license record exists of the inn as such until February 11, 1819, when John Borradaile and his wife Jane, of Haddonfield, Gloucester County, sold "*to Isaac Smith of Galloway Township and James Smith . . . for $400.00 . . . all that certain Tavern House and lot of land . . . in Smithville, . .*"

However, a Road Return of March 1812 mentions "A Public Inn kept by Enos Smith of Galloway Township." Architectural details of the original building of the Smithville Inn reflect eighteenth century construction: the Jersey stone foundation, wrought iron nails, split plaster lath, "HL" hinges on doors.

Isaac Smith obtained the Smithville Inn in late 1819 and operated the hostelry until 1837, when ownership was transferred to Henry Smith, who maintained it until 1865. The Smithville Inn soon thereafter was converted to a private dwelling, and so remained until 1952 when it was purchased and restored as an inn.

Although it has been enlarged considerably, to accommodate the larger number of travelers on the road today, great care has been taken to preserve the atmosphere of colonial South Jersey, and it is the only inn of its period still operating in this area after a century and a half.

The grounds surrounding the Smithville Inn have been developed as a composite historical South Jersey village. A grist mill with water wheel; a church, the Joslin Chapel; general store; candy shop; tobacconist; dwelling houses; all have been transported to Smithville and carefully restored. They have been opened and are operating, offering the same services as they did more than a century ago.

Before their relocation and restoration, not one of these places was available to the public, and many were in imminent danger of being destroyed for any one of many reasons.

The Smithville Inn today has succeeded in preserving much that reflects the life of historic Down Jersey.

* Recorded in Historic American Buildings Survey, Library of Congress

Indian Cabin Inn

Located on the Hammonton–Pleasant Mills Road four miles east of the White Horse Pike at the junction of Columbia Road.

ITS WEATHERED clapboards are hidden beneath modern asbestos siding; the roof is now of tar shingles; the wayfaring stranger no longer pauses. The sign of the Indian Cabin Mill has vanished . . . the inn that served so well from 1779 to 1864 has ceased to exist as such.

This was the inn that gained a reputation when in 1781 the noted refugee Tory outlaw Joseph Mulliner was captured there, according to legend, after a lifetime of terrorizing the Pine Barrens — robbing stages, burning farms, and aiding the British. But that is another story.

The Indian Cabin Mill Inn, at Indian Cabin, called later New Columbia, and now Nesco, like its counterparts of the era, had its tiny rooms for sleeping on the second floor; its several fireplaces for maintaining warmth during the long cold winters; beaded ceiling beams; and pegged mortise and tenon joinings of the beams, joists, and rafters — all typical of eighteenth-century Down Jersey buildings.

John Shane appears to have been the first to hold a license for this inn, having been taxed in 1779 for an inn *"between the Forks and Egg Harbour."* Shane held the license in 1781, the year Mulliner was finally seized.

The next account shows Richard Davis holding forth here about 1791 and then Henry Davis in 1803; and his will records Henry Davis is located "where John Shane formerly lived." Nothing has been found of the activities of the inn dur-

ing this period. In 1826, however, the following application was made during the June term of Court:

"The petition of William Erwin of the Township of Galloway . . . most respectfully sheweth That your petitioner hath taken rent and occupied all that Establishment formerly known by the name of Indian Cabin Mill in the Township . . . and is known by the name of Indian Cabin Mill, . . your petitioner being desirious to accommodate the traveler as well as the Inhabitants of the Township. . . . Therefore prays that the Honorable Court will be pleased to grant to your petitioner their license to keep said establishment as an Inn and Tavern. . . ."

The succession of ownership continued through the years: Harriet Erwin took over in 1827; Sherman Clark in 1828 to 1831; Edward Cline was licensed in 1832; William Wescoat held the place from 1835 to at least 1837. Records from then to 1861 have not been located, but in that year John Abbott became the owner and called the place the "Union Hotel," a popular name in those early days of the Civil War. Robert Brown took title to the place in 1864 and held it until after 1875.

The sign proclaiming the Union Hotel still exists, and is being safeguarded by the present owner of the Indian Cabin Mills Inn–Union Hotel, Mrs. William Brown. The old inn is now a private residence and all signs of its early life are hidden in the dust of time, but its history remains, forever.

"Joe Mulliner - Hung 1781"

*Tombstone found on Pleasant Mills—Weekstown Road, Route 43,
2.0 miles east of Pleasant Mills, on south side of road.*

A JERSEY NOR'EASTER was drenching the Pine Barrens as the Tuckerton stage left the warmth of the Quaker Bridge Tavern. Its driver fastened his cloak tightly about his neck, cracked his whip sharply over the team of horses, and gave them their heads down the narrow, winding, muddy rutted road to Batsto and the coast.

A scant mile or two would soon bring them near the Cold Spring Swamp, a dense, impassable cedar jungle overgrown with rhododendron and brier, populated by deer, bear, wildcat, and . . . Joseph Mulliner and his renegade band of Tory refugees.

Refugees! Men who voiced loyalty to the English Crown, but who in reality were bands of outlaws. Their raids threw terror into the hearts of true Jerseymen. They plundered and burned farmhouses, waylaid horsemen, kidnaped and ransomed, and held up stagecoaches.

Mulliner was the most famous — or infamous — of the refugee leaders. A swashbuckling Englishman with notorious good looks and a liking for music, drink, and dancing that would one day prove his undoing, Mulliner was known to lead a band of nearly a hundred men into every corner of Burlington and old Gloucester counties.

A fallen pine across the road brought the stage driver from his daydreaming. He reined the coach to a halt and prepared to dismount.

As he touched the ground a score of men materialized from the dense pines, their swords drawn and flintlocks cocked. A tall man in something of a uniform, with two large pistols tucked in a wide belt, strode forward and, with a deep hearty laugh, ordered the passengers to the ground.

The hapless victims of the South Jersey stage robbery knew there was no mistaking the refugee band and its leader as they melted into the twilight and rain-swept woods—Joe Mulliner had robbed another stage.

Weeks later, the widow Bates returned from Sunday services at Elijah Clark's Little Log Meeting House at The Forks (Pleasant Mills) to find a band of refugees plundering her home.

The men were loading a wagon with pigs, poultry, grain stores, and her house furnishings, including some heirloom silverware. As the widow Bates saw this she gathered her four young sons close to her and opened up on the outlaws with a verbal barrage.

One of the refugees ordered her to be silent or her house would be burned to the ground, whereupon the good widow Bates replied, "T'would be an act worthy of cowardly curs like you, you may burn my house but my tongue will never stop as long as there's breath in my body."

One of the refugees lifted a flaming log from the fireplace hearth and set a corner of the house ablaze. As her boys attempted to pelt the refugees with stones, the widow Bates tried to douse the fire with water, but the outlaws grabbed them, lashed them to trees, and permitted the home to burn to the ground.

Although Mulliner was not with the band, they were recognized as members of his gang. Legend states Mulliner was in this case disturbed by the actions of his men, who apparently acted without his authorization. An anonymous donation of some three hundred dollars several weeks later to the widow Bates is said to have come from Mulliner.

The stories of Joseph Mulliner are many, his exploits along the Mullica as wild, exciting, and romantic as any fiction. But the noose was slowly tightening as one evening he stepped into an inn at Indian Cabin (Nesco, near Pleasant Mills). A score of couples were dancing to the tune of a fiddler, and other couples were singing gaily. The festivities stopped as Mulliner joined the group of merrymakers.

His eyes swept the scene. Flickering candles revealed uncertainty, even fear, in the faces of the citizens. The fiddler slowly laid his instrument on the floor. Over at one side of the room the fireplace continued to shed the only warmth now in the room.

But Mulliner shouted, "Music, and let's dance! And a tankard of ale!" Hesitatingly, the fiddler took his bow and bent to the strings. The dancing resumed, but without its former gusto. The refugee leader strode into the throng and, pushing a young man aside, started dancing with his girl — the best-looking girl present.

Minutes later, the furious man slipped outside, past a couple of guards posted by Mulliner, and sped to the home of Captain Baylin, chief of the local militia, who had long sought the king of the refugees. An old Indian fighter, Baylin had dedicated himself to Mulliner's capture.

The militiaman rallied a posse and converged on the inn, seizing the notorious Tory bandit.

The *New Jersey Gazette* of August 8, 1781, reported: *"At a special court lately held in Burlington, a certain Joseph Mulliner, of Egg-Harbour, was convicted of high treason, and is sentenced to be hanged this day. This fellow had become the terror of that part of the country. He had made a practice of burning houses, robbing and plundering all who fell in his way, so that when he came to trial it appeared that the whole country, both whigs and tories, were his enemies."*

Mulliner was taken from the goal, placed in a wagon with his own coffin, taken to a point called Gallows Hill, and there hanged.

His body was sent by wagon along the very route he terrorized, to his wife at Sweetwater, where he was buried along a high bank overlooking the Mullica River and the Cold Spring Swamp. His epitaph is there today to see: "Grave of Joe. Mulliner — Hung — 1781."

The Shaler Grave

Located on Indian Cabin Cabin Road, 0.5 miles east of Philadelphia Avenue, Egg Harbor, at northeast corner of the Park lake, about 50 feet in woods from bend of road.

SIBBEL SHALER, who rests now in the pines in a common grave with three of her infant children, was the wife of one of the more noted privateer captains to sail the Jersey coast.

Timothy, Master in 1782 of the galley *Alligator*, a vessel owned by Joseph Ball of Batsto, as well as of many other craft that had engaged in privateering ventures, made the Forks and Chestnut Neck his headquarters for many daring exploits and engagements that resulted in the seizure of prizes.

Folklore claims that Mrs. Shaler and her children were massacred by Indians during one of her husband's many voyages, but reliable aboriginal records of New Jersey fail to reveal a single case of an Indian massacre in the history of the Province.

What caused the simultaneous deaths of Timothy Shaler's family is open to speculation, but it could have been the accidental burning of their home, or disease.

47

Atlantic County Court House

The historic Atlantic County Courthouse is located in the center of Mays Landing, at the junction of Route 50 and Main Street.

DR. JONATHAN PITNEY left his seat in the high ladder-back rocker. Fingering his favorite pipe, he drew a puff and turned to his companion across the room. The two men, old-time friends, had been discussing the forthcoming division of Gloucester County, and the creation of a new county along the coastal plain from the eastern portion of old Gloucester. Pitney was about to leave, their talk concluded.

Judge Daniel Baker of Bakersville (now Northfield) grasped the latch and opened the door wide. The crisp air of the winter of 1837 filled the room. Creation of the new county was the news of the day.

"Daniel," said Pitney, "what name shall we give our new county?"

His honor, who was peering out the door and over the salt marshes toward Absecon Island and the Atlantic Ocean, replied, "Doctor, there is the broad Atlantic Ocean, what name is more appropriate than Atlantic County?"

According to legend, this old Jersey stone building, on the River Road, one mile from central Mays Landing, housed the first Atlantic County jail.

48

Thus it was that on February 7, 1837, by an act of the State Legislature of New Jersey, Atlantic County was created from sprawling Gloucester, which at that time reached from the ocean to the Delaware River, including all of what today is Gloucester, Camden, and Atlantic counties.

Gloucester County then boasted a population of 28,431 persons, "including males, females and slaves." What was to be Atlantic County was populated by 8,164 of that number, far less than today's population of Pleasantville. The County Seat, Woodbury, was just too far from the coastal regions to provide effective administration of the region's affairs and growing problems.

Only four townships existed at the time in Atlantic County: Egg Harbor, Weymouth, Hamilton, and Galloway. Mullica Township was created later in 1838, from Galloway, and the town of Hammonton from Mullica and Hamilton in 1866. Buena Vista, in 1867, was created from Hamilton Township.

Among the cities of the county, Atlantic City, destined one day to be nicknamed the "World's Playground," was set apart from Egg Harbor Township in 1854. Egg Harbor City was incorporated in 1858 and Port Republic in 1905, from Galloway Township. Estell Manor was created from Weymouth Township in 1925, while Mays Landing dates before the creation of Atlantic County.

The first County Commissioners were Joseph Endicott, General Enoch Doughty, and Judge Daniel Baker. One of their first problems was the construction of a seat of government for the new county, and Mays Landing was chosen for its ideally central location.

Samuel Richards, proprietor of several iron furnaces and forges in the area, donated in May of 1838 the necessary land for county buildings, and the present courthouse and other structures were soon under construction. Sessions of court were held in the meantime at the hotel of Captain John Pennington, nearby.

Today, as in 1837, Mays Landing is an ideal setting for the Atlantic County government. The courthouse and buildings are historically significant and are located in a park, amidst towering trees that were but saplings when they were built.

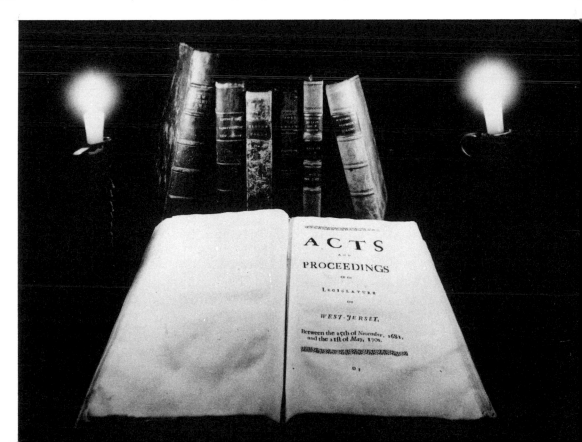

Eighteenth- and nineteenth-century books treating the history and laws of New Jersey and West Jersey. The opened work is Leaming and Spicer's Grants, Concessions and Constitution of New Jersey, of which 170 copies were printed in 1758.

West's Mystery at Catawba

*Family burial plot and mansion site is located on the May Landing–
Somers Point Road, Route 559, 3.6 miles east of Mays Landing on
the northerly side of the road.*

SOLITARY and broken, almost hidden by scrub oak, the grave marker of George West
at Catawba is all that remains of a strange tale of happiness and prosperity, tragedy
and mystery, dating from more than a century ago.

It was the late eighteenth century, and a prosperous Burlington County merchant moved
his family into Gloucester County and settled in a promising community of some size along
the Great Egg Harbor River. A beautiful mansion was constructed and furnished in elegant
style. Its site commanded a fine view of the river and the ships plying the coastal trade, with
Mays Landing their port of call.

Thus did George and Amy West come to Catawba, with little premonition of the terror
to strike their home a quarter-century later. The mystery and suspicion that followed were
to drive entire families from the community and turn the village into the ghost town it is today.

The skeleton in the West family closet was to be son Joseph, eldest of their three children. Although of excellent appearance and background, Joseph was to leave his mark as
one of the most hated, feared, and notorious characters in South Jersey.

His business dealings as a lawyer and surveyor were ruthless, and his extravagance and
arrogance caused difficulties that involved even the President of the United States.

50

The legend is told that the President (though it is not stated which one) traveled with four fine white horses and an outfitted coach. So did Joseph West . . . with four mules and a mulatto driver, and West made every effort to be as conspicuous as possible, even to the point of carrying silk bedclothes for his personal use when he stopped at inns and hotels.

The President wrote West, asking him to change his style of travel, but a second note was necessary before he would comply. West kept his promise then by driving three white horses and a white mule.

Disaster began to strike the West family. James West, aged nineteen, died on August 24, 1829; then George West, Jr., twenty-three, died just nine days later. George West, Esq. died seven days later on the 10th of September, and Amy West passed on only five days later. Their "illnesses" were of extremely short duration, and, being a family that enjoyed robust health, the curious passing of the prominent family was a strange occurrence . . . particularly since only son Joseph was to survive.

The passing of his parents and brothers left Joseph West in command of the family estate. But law enforcement techniques and personnel being at an absolute minimum, no investigation followed, and Joseph wrote flowery epitaphs, sealed the graves, closed the mansion, and vanished from the scene.

Neighbors believed the community cursed, and within months Catawba was a ghost village.

Legend has it that prior to Joseph West's departure he rigged a shotgun to the front door of the Catawba family mansion to do away with the first prowler to enter. Then many years later, finis was written to the story of Catawba when Joseph strangely reappeared and, forgetting his own trap, killed himself upon opening the door to the old homestead.

Fireplace mantle from the Wests' Mansion House at Catawba, now the property of Robert McMullin of Absecon

51

The One-Room Schoolhouse

Located on the north side of Mays Landing–Somers Point Road, 1.6 miles from Mays Landing at Clarkstown Road.

GRAVELLY RUN is a ghost town, a typical old forgotten village of South Jersey. The tavern, school, church, and many homes are abandoned, vanished, or decaying. The hamlet is still on the map, but in little more than name only.

Perched high on a hill, nearly hidden from the road by pines, stands the Gravelly Run School, built late in the nineteenth century and typical of the old Down Jersey one-room schoolhouses that once dotted the countryside. It is one of the few such buildings remaining, and the last known class was promoted in 1926, when the school children were transferred to Mays Landing.

Fourteen to thirty young Jerseymen received their education each year in the old school, and a single teacher, usually a man, taught as many as ten grades. Sometimes grades would have but a single student or two, yet everything from first grade reading to 10th grade arithmetic was taught.

Boys and girls used separate entrances to the single room and were seated in separate sections. Discipline was the order of the day, and when the occasion demanded, the teacher would not hesitate to administer a well-deserved whipping. Usually though, the more rambunctious boys would be brought into line by being made to endure the shame of sitting at a desk with a girl. Times have changed somewhat.

A cast iron pot-belly stove stood in one corner, and an organ in the other. Children sat at double desks facing the blackboard in front. Three high windows were on either side. A water bucket was placed in the back corner. The common tin cup was never dipped in the bucket. In an attempt to be sanitary, only the dipper was allowed to dip into the bucket and transfer the water to the tin cup.

A short way from the school stands two outside toilets with a high board fence separating the boy's side from the girl's side. A pump house was at the bottom of the hill. A belfry on top of the building holds the big bell which was rung by pulling a heavy rope which extended through the ceiling and dangled just within reach.

In the playground, boys and girls would sometimes join in such games as 'Duck-on-Davy,' a version of 'hide-go-seek,' and 'Pussy,' a game played by hitting a hand whittled peg with a stick as far as possible, and, while the person who was 'it' ran to retrieve it, the rest would run and hide. Another game, 'Landy Over,' was played by throwing a ball over the roof of the school. Players on the far side would catch it, run around the building and attempt to tag one of the opposing players, who would then have to change sides. If the throw or tag was missed, the players on the receiving end would yell 'Landy Over!' and toss the ball back for their opponents to try and snare.*

School days of a century ago in South Jersey's little one-room schoolhouses are only memories. Oil lamps, scarred desks, long benches, tattered dunce's caps, and outdoor conveniences are a far cry from today's elaborate educational plants.

Students of old South Jersey could seldom even ride a horse to school, although the daily walk might be a couple of miles or more, in all varieties of weather. And there was nothing like the cherry-red, glowing pot-belly stove "for a guy to back up to" and get warm for a moment before class.

Like many other of Atlantic County's historical treasures, the Gravelly Run School today is a victim of neglect; a local trace of America's heritage may soon disappear. Restoration of the Gravelly Run School would not *now* be difficult or expensive—*if* only there were a local group interested in such a monument to American education.

* Historic trip up Great Egg Harbor—Nickles—1956 MSS

Wreck of the Schooner Weymouth

*Located on the Clarktown Road, 1.3 miles south
of its junction with Mays Landing Road at Gravelly
Run Schoolhouse (visible only at very low tide).*

"BLOW-OUT" TIDES of the Great Egg Harbor River lay bare the gaunt ribs of the two-masted schooner *Weymouth*. She has lain in her watery grave for nearly seventy-five years, anchored fast in the sands and mud of the river bottom.

Captain Samuel Gaskill built the *Weymouth* at his Mays Landing shipyards in 1868. She was a small vessel, only 57.8 feet in length with a beam of some 20 feet and displacing 59.75 tons.

Sailing under the hand of Captain William Barrett of Mays Landing, the *Weymouth* was a merchant craft, carrying foods, household goods, farm implements, and other staples between Philadelphia, Mays Landing, and other points along the South Jersey coast. In later years she sailed under the command of Captain J. T. Coleman.

It is said the *Weymouth* met her end when, after having been retired from the sea and moored at the old Deal's Point wharf near Mays Landing, several boys slipped her lines for a prank and she drifted on a sand bar, where she remained.

However, a newspaper account of the vanishing shipbuilding industry in Atlantic County, published in 1914 when the incident was still fresh in the minds of residents, tells a different tale.

The *Weymouth* was returning to Mays Landing with a load of housewares from Philadelphia. Almost home, and opposite Clarktown, a sudden thunderstorm broke and the vessel was struck by lightning, toppling her rigging. Strong winds drove the hapless vessel hard and fast into shoal water where she stuck sufficiently hard to resist all attempts at salvage. Her cargo removed, she was abandoned.

Mays Landing, English Creek, Patcong Creek, Nacote Creek, Chestnut Neck, and villages along the Mullica River were bustling shipbuilding centers from the late eighteenth century up to and including, in some cases, the present time. Craft built in Atlantic County of old could and did ply the Seven Seas. Two-, three-, and even four-masted craft were commonplace, and the shipwrights had the finest of materials right at hand: oak and Jersey cedar, cut from trees five and six feet in diameter. Jersey bog iron, with its famed no-rust quality, came from the furnaces at Etna, Weymouth, Gloucester, and Batsto to provide nails, bolts, rings, and other fittings for the craft. Masts for early ships were cut in the area, but later, as the supply of suitable timber dwindled, masts were imported from the Carolinas and elsewhere.

George May at "the Landing" is known to have built craft prior to the Revolution. An early deed of February, 1767, contains the phrase *"near the shipyard,"* referring to land along Patcong Creek. It establishes Great Egg Harbor as an early shipbuilding center.

The *Olive,* a sloop skippered by Captain J. Bunker, appears in records of 1769, and Charles Steelman of Stephen's Creek built craft there before 1812. His

Gaunt ribs of the Weymouth, exposed at low tide

will, dated that year, mentions "one vessel on the stocks, and plank and timber in the shipyard."

When the final thud of the "corking" hammer sounded, the last coat of paint was applied, and the last splice in the rigging made, such ships as the three-master, 138.9 foot schooner *Amanda C. Parker;* Schooner *Annie S. Gaskill;* three-master *21 Friends;* the *John Shay;* Schooner *License;* and scores of others slid down the ways in the Great Egg Harbor.

But the Age of Steam was at hand. . . . Sailing vessels, once proud, graceful possessors of the sea were doomed by "progress." More than two hundred major vessels had been built in little more than a century in Atlantic County, at least half of them near Mays Landing.

Finally, in 1885, Captain Gaskill built the three-master *Edward G. Taulane,* last wood vessel to be launched in Mays Landing. When she hit the water at the foot of her ways, an era ended.

Old Country Churches

SURROUNDED by their silent, timeless congregations, South Jersey's old churches are a memorial to the past and a guidepost for the future. These gleaming white clapboard or red brick houses of worship were and are the backbone of life among the Jersey pines. Farmers, ironworkers, glass blowers, lawyers, doctors, and plantation masters became one on Sunday, then as they do now, when they would mount their horses, or bundle their families into carriages for the dusty ride to church.

They would come from every direction, responding to the clear, mellow tones of the church bell as it pealed its message across the rural countryside. A broiling summer sun or drifting winter snows were no deterrent to attendance at Sunday services.

Seldom could a church boast its own preacher; the congregations were just not large enough to support them. Accordingly, traveling ministers, called circuit riders, made the rounds of a series of churches, pausing at each to conduct services.

HEAD OF THE RIVER CHURCH
Tuckahoe Vicinity, New Jersey

Reining up before the church, the circuit preacher of long ago would dismount, and opening his saddle bags, remove his Bible and turn to greet his arriving parishioners.

Windows would be thrown open during summer months and the warm breeze may have made the congregation physically uncomfortable as they sat in the stiff board pews, but the exhortations of the preacher and the united hymn singing gave everyone a spiritual boost.

The circuit rider would lead his congregation in services that occasionally lasted for two or three hours. Then the Bible would be closed, and the preacher would pause on the steps to meet again his departing flock before he would mount his horse and ride on to the next charge.

Bishop Francis Asbury, Philip Vickers Fithian, Nicholas Collin, John and David Brainerd, Reverend Allen Brown, the Reverend Richard Sneath, were but a few of the famed religious men to visit and preach in the churches of South Jersey and coastal Gloucester County.

Pioneer stock of old Atlantic County in a religious sense were the Quakers, who organized several meetings in coastal villages. Earliest of these was the Meeting at Somerset Plantation, the home of John Somers, about 1695. This was later held alternately at Somerset (Somers Point) and across the river in Cape May County.

When Richard Somers built the brick mansion at Somerset about 1726, the locale of the meetings was changed to the new building, his residence. Crossing the Great Egg Harbor River sometimes presented problems for Friends living on the opposite side from the Meeting place when the waters were rough. They oftentimes were able to use the ferry from Job's Point to Beesley's Point, but sometimes were forced to resort to canoes or flat-bottom boats. One boat, reserved for Friends Meetings was called "the business boat."

This was, however, an improvement over the fortune of Quakers attending the Meetings at Tuckerton, traveling from old Atlantic County, they were forced to swim the Little Egg Harbor River for want of a better means of crossing. The spot chosen for this usually dangerous task was a half mile east of the present bridges over the river, at an area where the river is only an eighth of a mile wide. The crossing became known as "Swimming Over Point." This method of crossing the river was continued for many years until several members drowned in the swift waters of the river.

By 1726, three places were used by the Friends for Meetings. Japhet Leeds's at Leedspoint, Peter White's at Absecon, and Somerset Plantation.

In earliest times the churches were of simple architecture, and unadorned. First among these houses of worship in colonial times, were the Little Log Meeting House in Pleasant Mills, built in 1762 by Elijah Clark, and a similar structure in Absecon, predecessor of the Methodist Church there.

By the last decade of the eighteenth century, the buildings were more pretentious. Head of the River Methodist Church is a fine wood clapboard building built in 1792, shortly after the first Methodist Church in America was constructed in Philadelphia.

After the turn of the nineteenth century, the churches continued in a more elaborate style. Fine clapboard buildings that still remain today were built at Pleasant Mills, Friendship, Estellville, and Mays Landing. A handsome red brick edifice at Bargaintown was built in 1822.

Church building in the 1860's assumed a more elaborate, and what has become a more traditional style, with tall spires reaching to the skies. The Absecon Presbyterian Church and the Port Republic Methodist Church were erected during this era. In our story to follow, we shall trace the history of these.

Today some of these early churches have vanished. Others remain, with congregations to open their doors but once a year, on the anniversary of their founding. Their congregations rest silently in the churchyard, their stone markers a church history in granite.

∧ The silent congregation—wooden markers at Pleasant Mills

58

The silent congregation—bog iron markers at Weymouth

The silent congregation—stone markers at Stephen's Creek

Resting place of sea captains, Revolutionary soldiers, and privateers

Smith's Meeting House Site

Situated on the south side of Main Street, east of Mill Road in Port Republic.

THIS IS THE SITE of the Methodist Union Chapel at Blackman's Mills, in Port Republic incorporated in 1837. It was built at the turn of the eighteenth century by Micajah Smith, a sea captain and privateer master, overlooking Nacote Creek.

Old State historical marker at meeting house site

SMITH'S MEETING HOUSE
Built by Micajah Smith about 1800. Named "Methodist Union Chapel at Blackman's Mills" when incorporated in 1837. Micajah Smith, John Van Sant, Privateer Captains, and Jonas Morse and James Bell, Revolutionary soldiers, are buried in the Church Yard.
THE NEW JERSEY COMMISSION ON HISTORIC SITES

Clark's Mills Meeting House

*Located on Indian Cabin Road, 0.5 miles from the paved
road from Port Republic to English Creek. Indian Cabin
Road is 0.6 from Port Republic's Mill Road.*

CLARK'S MILL BRANCH of Nacote Creek wound past a mill, a tavern, a number of dwellings, and a Meeting House, comprising a village by the same name that one day would become Wrangleboro, then Unionville, and finally Port Republic.

Built in 1762, Clark's Mills Meeting House was another of the Reverend John Brainerd's churches, and though it served the area until 1820, it is believed to have been destroyed in a windstorm that year.

Reverend Brainerd, in his Journal under the date of February 23, 1761, stated he *"preached a lecture at Chestnut Neck. After sermon stayed the heads or principle members of the congregation to discourse about building a meeting house."* This undoubtedly was to be the church at Clark's Mills, two miles distant.

Philip Vickers Fithian, Presbyterian preacher of Greenwich, Cumberland County, and noted circuit rider of the day, visited Egg Harbor in 1775, and notes in his Journal that *"he preached at Clark's Mills Meeting House to an attentive assembly on Monday, February 27, . . ."*

Today all that remains to mark the site is a burying ground. Here rest Adrial, Parker, and Thomas Clark, Revolutionary soldiers. Six other members of the Clark family served in the Revolution, and are probably buried here, but inscriptions on the markers, victims of time and the weather, have vanished.

61

Port Republic Methodist Church

Located on Main Street, center of village

METHODISM BEGAN in Port Republic in 1796, a result of the preachings there of Bishop Francis Asbury, first Methodist Bishop of America. One of the early church leaders was Nehemiah Blackman, one of the Bishop's first converts.

The Reverend Richard Sneath, in his diary notes: *"1799. April 3 — preached at Rangleborough and had a very good time the people were considerably engaged in the evening had prayer meeting at Esqr Smiths but not so lively as sometimes it has been."* A later account states: *"1800. March 25, crossed the river and went to see my old friends at Wrangleboro i preached to them at 11 and had a powerful time, in evening held meeting at Br Collins which was attended with power."*

Captain Micajah Smith presented a parcel of land about 1800 for *"a meeting house and burying ground."* This became known as "Smith's Meeting House and Burying Ground" (see page 60), and the Society of Methodists erected a modest church. Smith, a privateer skipper of considerable note, is buried there with John VanSant, privateer captain, and Jonas Morse and James Bell, Revolutionary soldiers.

The Society at Port Republic, by then called Unionville, was incorporated in 1837, and the church called the Methodist Union Chapel. Among the trustees were Nehemiah Blackman, Nicholas VanSant, Gilbert Hatfield, Ralph Ashley, Joseph Garwood, Levi Howard, and Abner Gaskill. Five of VanSant's sons became ministers, and a sixth, John, traveled to Minnesota, later to become Governor of the State.

Unionville—Port Republic—was a part of the Bargaintown Circuit until it joined the Absecon Circuit in 1854, when its membership had reached two hundred and thirty. The small church continued in use until after the Civil War, when, in 1870, a huge revival began, under the Reverend W. T. Randolph, resulting in the erection of the present edifice, known today as the Port Republic Methodist Church, and nicknamed by many, "The Christmas Card Church," because of its grace and beauty.

Emmaus Methodist Church

*Situated on Moss Mill Road, 0.2 miles east
of Route 9, Shore Road, in Smithville.*

THE FIRST METHODIST Class or Society was formed at Smithville, or Leeds as the hamlet was sometimes called, in 1796–97, and the first Meeting House built there at the corner of Morse Mill Road and Old King's Highway. The church was a part of the Bargaintown Circuit until 1854, when it joined the Absecon Circuit.

Reverend Richard Sneath entered in his diary: *"1798. July 22—preached at Leeds at 3 nothing in particular."* Later, on December 9th, he mentions: *". . . the storm kept me from going to Leeds in the afternoon."* These entries prove the existence of a Society in that year.

The present church building was constructed in 1869.

Earlier, though, on April 16, 1854, the ship *Powhatan*, carrying three hundred and eleven German emigrants, was wrecked in a violent storm above Atlantic City, with the loss of all lives. Bodies were found for weeks along the coastal beaches, and buried at the nearest cemeteries. Fifty-four victims were laid to rest in a common trench grave in the Smithville Church burying ground in a section called the "Friends Cemetery."

The second oldest Friends Meeting House in old Atlantic County was built near the present church building between 1744 and 1752, and one Japhet Leeds was appointed overseer.

Hosea Joslin's Chapel

Located on the grounds of Smithville Inn, Route 9, Shore Road, at Smithville.

HOSEA JOSLIN, licensed as an Exhorter in 1825, was a member of the Methodist Society in Mays Landing, and continued in that post for fifty-five years. During his tenure, he built a small chapel at Sugar Hill, less than a mile east of the Landing, about the year 1850.

Records of the Salem Quarterly Meeting show a Methodist Society at Joyslin's (Joslin's) as early as 1789.

The chapel at Sugar Hill was moved to the Union Cemetery on the Somers Point Road shortly after Joslin's death in 1880, where it remained, unused in recent years and falling victim to the elements, until it was moved in 1961 to Smithville and restored.

Absecon Methodist Church

Located on corner of Church Street and Pitney Road, in Absecon.

ABSECON BECAME part of Salem Circuit when, in 1796–97 a Methodist revival resulted in the forming of classes in the village. Under the guidance of the Reverend John Mc-Clasky, and two noted circuit riding preachers, Anthony Turk and Richard Sneath, the new Society flourished, and soon outgrew the modest church built in the late eighteenth century for the flock.

The village joined the Gloucester Circuit in 1813, and a decade later the growing pains brought the congregation together in a united effort to construct a new edifice. With care, the following words were noted in the Church's constitution:

"We the people of Absecon and Vicinity at a public meeting held in the Meeting House, in Absecon, on 3rd day of March A.D. 1823, pursuant to the Act of Assembly of the State of New Jersey for incorporating Religious Societies in order to the more effectually to accommodate ourselves and our posterity with a house in which we may more quietly assemble to worship Almighty God, have agreed to build a house for that purpose. . . ."

Thus it was that in 1829, a year after becoming part of the Bargaintown Circuit, with Charles Pitman, Presiding Elder, John Walker, and James Ayres, Circuit Preachers, the present building was proudly dedicated. Although rebuilt in 1856, the superb architecture of the building caused the U.S. Department of the Interior to record the structure in the Historic American Buildings Survey.

"The first Methodist Meeting House was located on old King's Highway a quarter mile northeast of the present church. Built under a Mr. Locke, a Baptist minister from Cape May, it boasted a wood ceiling, rather than the customary plaster. Robert Doughty, a ruling Elder of the Clark's Mill Presbyterian Church was the chief builder, and when completed had a gallery on two sides and the rear."

Absecon Presbyterian Church

Located on New Jersey Avenue near School Street.

T HE PRESBYTERY of West Jersey had been formed in 1839, and in 1854 the organization appointed the Reverend Allen Brown as its missionary in South Jersey. Having come to old Atlantic County some years earlier, in 1846, the Reverend Mr. Brown had made his home in Absecon.

The earliest meetings of village Presbyterians were held in the Odd Fellows Hall on Church Street. This, however, proved unsatisfactory, and the urge for a formal church building was soon felt. By 1856 the congregation's Board of Trustees had purchased a four-acre tract of land for an edifice and burying ground.

Three years later, following a sermon by Reverend Brown, and in the presence of Daniel Townsend, ruling Elder of the Leeds Point Presbyterian Church, the Presbyterian Church of Absecon was organized, with only eight persons: George and Frances Scott, Felix and Eunice Leeds, Janet Farish, John Weber, Rebecca W. Doughty, and Hannah H. Doughty.

It was not until June of 1865 that the trustees were able to build their church. The cornerstone was laid on November 16 and construction was under way. Three months later the Reverend Charles T. McMullin became the first installed pastor of the church.

And less than two years later, on June 20, 1867, the Absecon Presbyterian Church was dedicated, free of debt.

Mays Landing Presbyterian Church

Located corner Route 50 and Main Street, Northwest.

PRESBYTERIANS living at the County Seat of the young Atlantic County laid the cornerstone for their church in 1841, on lands donated by Samuel Richards, proprietor of the iron furnaces at Weymouth and Atsion. By October 1842, the congregation was conducting services.

The Reverend Samuel L. Colt was minister from 1842 to 1846. Following his service, in 1866, a school was opened under the church's sponsorship. A fee of fifty dollars was charged by A. M. Girault, Jr., the teacher, for an eleven-week term.

The architectural importance of the Mays Landing Presbyterian Church resulted in the U.S. Department of the Interior including the building in the Historic American Buildings Survey Archives at the Library of Congress, in the 1930's.

Weymouth Methodist Church

Located 0.5 miles north of Weymouth Road on gravel road, enter this unpaved road 1.0 mile east of Weymouth Road junction and Black Horse Pike.

THE WEYMOUTH Methodist Meeting House stands today, as it has for one hundred and seventy years, in a pleasant oak grove almost on the banks of the Great Egg Harbor River. Built in 1807 primarily for the ironworkers at Weymouth Furnace by its proprietor, Samuel Richards, the church is still used today for services on the Sabbath.

Fastened chiefly with wooden pegs, the modest clapboard building with the old church bell on its peak has served through the rise and decline of the village, from iron furnace to paper mill and, finally now, to just a rural community lacking even a post office.

Originally, the Weymouth Furnace Company granted both Methodists and Presbyterians use of the building and cemetery, and services were held on alternate Sundays. Both denominations shared in the upkeep.

In 1845 the Class Leader was one James Campbell (Cambell). He was succeeded in 1850 by Peter McCollum. A William Muskelly took charge in 1851, followed by Robert Love in 1852. One Charles E. S. Mayhew was Exhorter in 1850.

Grave markers cast of Jersey bog iron, probably at nearby Weymouth Furnace, stand side by side with century-old wooden markers and more recent stone markers. True to its reputation, the bog iron has not rusted, although to judge by the date thereon, the markers have been exposed to the weather for at least one hundred and twenty-five years.

71

Zion Meeting House

Situated on Zion Road, Bargaintown, 0.3 miles south of Parkway overpass.

A DECADE BEFORE the Revolutionary War, in 1764, Jerseymen at Bargaintown established the Cedar Bridge Meeting House. It was a Presbyterian congregation until 1814, and was visited by the most noted circuit riding ministers of the day, the Reverends John Brainerd and Philip Vickers Fithian.

Andrew Blackman, who was destined to serve in the Revolution, presented the original deed to the congregation, and the founding fathers of the church included two others, Joseph Scull and Joseph Ingersoll, who were later to serve during the War for Independence.

"1775, Saturday 25th — From the Forks of Little Egg Harbour I rode to the sea shore to Mr. Price's, an English young gentleman of fortune and breeding, with a desire to preach still lower down"—and the diary of Philip Vickers Fithian continues: *"Sunday 26. I preached to a thin assembly at Cedar Bridge Meeting House."*

Cedar Bridge, called also Blackman's Meeting House, was set back from the main road, and built of wood "board and batten" construction. By 1789 it was a part of the Salem Circuit and contributed sixteen shillings, eight pence to the Quarterly Conference that year.

After the turn of the century, Methodists in the region began using the Meeting House for services, a custom reflected elsewhere in old Gloucester County. Bishop Francis Asbury preached in Blackman's in 1809. And by 1814 the Methodist Society, having no permanent church, resolved to form a permanent congregation and purchase the Meeting House. On October 31 of that year the plan became a reality.

The congregation swiftly outgrew their church, and in 1822 a fine red brick edifice was built near the old church and near the road. One of the subscribers for the new building was Levi Price, Sr., a member of the crew of the United States Frigate *Constitution*.

The deed for the lands of the new church were given by Joseph Sharp, Esq., and his wife Hannah of Galloway Township, Gloucester County, for the consideration of twenty-five dollars. The new Meeting was called Zion, and in 1828 became part of the Bargaintown Circuit. Among the early preachers were Walter Burrows and James Moore.

Although in 1853 there were but forty-eight members of the church on the official rolls, the congregation apparently grew and flourished, for today the Zion Meeting House in Bargaintown is still very active and services are held weekly.

Eleven Revolutionary War soldiers rest in the burying grounds that surround the Zion Meeting House on all sides. They include John Tilton, Zephaniah Steelman, Joseph Scull, Abel Scull, Edward Risley, Thompson Price, John Jeffers, Nicholas Frambes, Andrew Frambes, David Blackman, and John Baker.

Asbury Methodist Church

Situated on Asbury Avenue, east side of road,
0.2 miles north of Zion Road in English Creek.

A LOG CABIN provided meeting facilities for early Methodists in English Creek. Called in the eighteenth century, "Englishes," the congregation was on the Salem Circuit. Records in the Salem Quarterly Meeting of 1789 show a contribution of sixteen shillings, eleven pence from "Inglishe's."

"July 13, 1798—preached at Englishes had a very powerful time joined 2 in class the work is prosperous here." The Reverend Richard Sneath, Circuit Preacher, continued his Journal: *"August 17, 1798—preached at Englishes some disturbance among the people has cast a damp upon them."* Then, *"December 7, 1798—haveing an appointment at Englishes this day i hurried for an early start but the river being full of ice it was difficult getting along it was after ten when we landed yet i made the place before the people scatered i made an appointment and preached in the evening at Blackman's."*

A Society of Methodists was organized in 1827, and held meetings in a building known as the English Meeting House. In February of that year, James and Mary English gave a deed to the church for one acre of ground, but for a now unknown purpose.

By 1850 the church, with eighty-nine members, had become part of the Bargaintown Circuit, and in 1852 a new building was erected to provide for the needs of the congregation. A decade later disaster struck, and the structure was burned to the ground.

Reconstruction began immediately, under the guidance of Reverend Edwin Water, and in 1863 the present edifice was dedicated.

The old slave
gallery

The Friendship Methodist Church (page 76); an interior scene from the pulpit (page 77)

Narrow, almost
straight-backed
pews in the gallery
were not designed
for comfort

78

Friendship Methodist Church

Situated on Weymouth Road at junction of Friendship Road,
on outskirts of Landisville.

IT WAS AN AREA of nearly unbroken wilderness, a scattering of houses, and but a few small industries—lumber, tar, and charcoal among them—when a handful of Methodist families settled in the then Weymouth Township in the late eighteenth century. Under the leadership of exhorters and local preachers, religious services were held in the homes of the people until 1808, when the present edifice was constructed.

William and Hope Hollingshead were the original owners and donors of the land, presenting it to the congregation for one dollar on May 14, 1808. The new church became part of the Gloucester Circuit, and the first preacher there was the Circuit riding minister, the Reverend Richard Sneath. It is now on the Bridgeton Circuit.

Early members of the Board of Trustees included John Smith, Joel Stewart, William Ackley, John Veal, John Smith, Jr., George Smith, and Thomas Champion.

The building was constructed using 6x14-inch hand-hewn timbers for supporting members. Foot-square wood pillars then supported the gallery, which remained unfinished until 1853, when the entire structure was repaired and reconstructed. The fine old high pulpit, with a flight of steps leading up each side to its platform, and enclosed with doors, was replaced at that time by an elevated stage. The "oval" ceiling was changed to a conventional flat plaster ceiling.

The exterior of the church was repaired in 1893, and periodically repairs were made. Despite the minor changes wrought over the years, electricity was not installed until 1958.

Friendship Church, situated in a picturesque grove of hardwoods, continues to hold services each Sabbath, and fortunately remains today, one of the least-changed old churches of Atlantic County.

Head of the River Church

Located on Route 49 at junction of County roads
66 and 49; about 4 miles from Tuckahoe.
(See color photograph—page 57)

THE OLDEST church building remaining in Atlantic County is the venerable old Head of the River edifice at the southern end of the county near Tuckahoe. Built in 1792 at the head of the Tuckahoe River in the then Weymouth Township, it was undoubtedly dedicated by Benjamin Abbott who traveled the Salem Circuit.

Bishop Francis Asbury states in his Journal that he visited the congregation in 1784, prior to construction of the church building, and made a return visit in 1809. The Reverend Mr. James was the first preacher to visit the Tuckahoe area.

The church, built on lands donated by Daniel Benezet, was constructed of timber cut in the area. Pine slab seats served worshipers, who assembled about the high pulpit, now modernized, which commanded a full view of the galleries around the sides and rear of the tiny room.

Head of the River Church served the workers at nearby Etna and Ingersoll iron furnaces, and the village at Etna boasted some forty families during its operation.

Eight Revolutionary War soldiers rest in the huge burying ground that surrounds the old church. They include John Champion, Joseph Estell, Lieutenant Joseph Ingersoll, John Mackey, David Sayres, Jeremiah Smith, Jonas Steelman, and David Weatherby.

Head of the River is one of three old Atlantic County churches that are judged to be of unusual historic and architectural importance by the U.S. Department of the Interior, and included by the National Park Service in the Historic American Buildings Survey Archives in the Library of Congress.

⟨ Interior of the Head of the River Church, showing oil lamps, pews, gallery and pulpit.

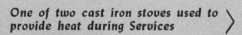

One of two cast iron stoves used to ⟩
provide heat during Services

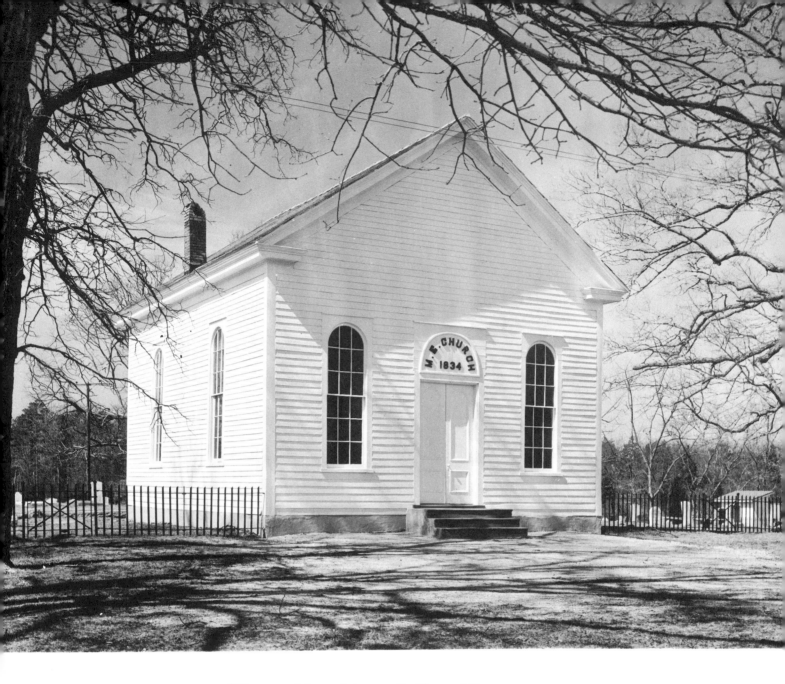

Estellville M. E. Church

Situated at the junction of Maple Avenue and Walkers Forge (Forty-Wire) Road, 0.3 miles west of Route 50 in Estellville.

THE ESTELLVILLE Methodist Episcopal Church was built in 1834 on lands donated by John Estell, and served primarily the religious needs of the workers at nearby Estellville Glassworks. Daniel Estell was among the early trustees of the church.

Records of the Bargaintown Circuit of 1845 reveal the Estells had two Classes with forty-six members, with one Somers S. Townsend the Leader of Class Number 1 and John Mart the leader of Class Number 2.

By April of 1850, Estellville had two Classes with a membership of seventy-six. Harbour Hughes, Somers Townsend, Elva D. Sise, and Edmund Scull were Leaders at that time.

Services are now held but once a year at the old Estellville Church, on the anniversary of its founding.

St. Mary's R.C. Church

*Site located on Pleasant Mills Road, north side, 1.3
miles east of Route 542, outskirts of Pleasant Mills.*

ST. MARY'S of the Assumption Roman Catholic Church, built in 1827, was the second church to be built in the Diocese of Trenton, which at the time included all of South Jersey. It is believed to have been the third Catholic Church in New Jersey, and was the first south of Trenton.

Prior to its erection, the nearest Catholic Church to Pleasant Mills and Atlantic County was in Philadelphia, thirty-five miles of sand roads and a ferry ride distant.

Jesse Richards, an Episcopalian and proprietor of the Batsto Furnace, donated the land for the church to his Catholic employees and assisted them in the building program. Protestant workers attended services at the nearby Pleasant Mills Church.

The Reverend Edward R. Mayne was the first pastor of St. Mary's, and the church flourished for thirty years, until 1860. By that time, the fires at the furnace had been out for twelve years, the cotton mill at Pleasant Mills had burned out, and the congregation had largely moved away. The final mass was celebrated with only eleven persons present.

The final chapter was written in April of 1900, when a forest fire swept the area, burning the small church to the ground. Today, only the burying ground remains. Here are buried Franz and Mary Froehlinger, parents of Joseph Fralinger, originator of Atlantic City's salt water taffy candy.

Pleasant Mills-Batsto Church

Situated at the "T" intersection of County Roads
542 and 43, in village of Pleasant Mills.

CLARK'S LITTLE LOG Meeting House, a tiny church of hand-hewn logs and cedar shingles, was built at the Forks, Pleasant Mills, in 1762, by Colonel Elijah Clark, who presented it to his neighbors. The building replaced an even earlier church that was built in 1758 and used variously by preachers of all denominations.

The Reverend John Brainerd, a close friend of Colonel Clark, was a frequent visitor to the chapel "in the wildwood," and an entry in his Journal of April 26, 1762, states that he *"preached for the first time in the new Meeting House at the Forks."* Philip Vickers Fithian refers often in his Journal and letters to Clark's Log Meeting House and his visits to the place. At the occasional times when no traveling preacher was available, Colonel Clark himself would lead the services.

When Charles Read established the iron furnace at nearby Batsto Village, the church began serving an increasingly large membership. Soon after the turn of the century, however, the growing pains forced Simon Lucas, former Revolutionary War

Captain of the Gloucester Militia, and pastor of the Little Log Meeting House, to consider construction of a larger church, and in 1808 the work began.

It was a proud day, that April 21 in 1809 when Bishop Francis Asbury dedicated the new church edifice. The Bishop records in his Journal of that day: *"At the Forks on Friday, I preached in our elegant chapel, on John XII. . . ."* This church remains today, enjoying services each Sabbath, in a picturesque setting that has changed little in one hundred and fifty years.

Wooden grave markers of South Jersey cedar, iron markers of native bog ore, and stone monuments note the resting places of generations of the church's congregation in the surrounding churchyard.

Huge cedars shade the graves of Captain Lucas, Jesse Richards, owner of Batsto Furnace, and members of his family. Nicholas Sooy, also a soldier in Washington's army during the Revolutionary War, and many veterans of the War Between the States rest here.

Grave of Jesse Richards, Iron maker (left); close-up of Henderson grave (right)

86   *Four huge cedars stand as silent sentinels at the corners of the century-old grave of Mary Henderson (page 84)*

Pleasant Mills Church today, a mirror of the past (page 85)

Kate Aylesford Mansion

Situated on Pleasant Mills Road, 0.2 miles east of Route 542, village of Pleasant Mills.

THIS WAS actually the home of Colonel Elijah Clark, public figure during colonial times, builder with Colonel Richard Wescoat of Fox Burrows Fort at Chestnut Neck, and member of the Provincial Congress of New Jersey in 1775.

The plot of a romantic Revolutionary War novel by Charles Peterson, written in 1856, entitled *Kate Aylesford,* was developed around a mythical heroine from England who was shipwrecked en route to America at Little Egg Harbor. After a dramatic rescue by the fictional Major Gordon, she resided in Pleasant Mills. Peterson's description of her home at the village tallies with Colonel Clark's home of the day, and, since 1856, the house has been nicknamed the "Kate Aylesford Mansion."

Today, it is the restored residence of Mr. and Mrs. Raymond Baker, and the cedar shingle roof, beaded clapboards, old window glass, and wooden shutters, viewed through huge old spruce trees, mirror the past at the village of the Forks.

The Old Absecon Light

Located at Rhode Island Avenue and Pacific Avenue in Atlantic City

GALE FORCE WINDS lashed the waters of the Atlantic along the South Jersey coast to the point of fury. Driving snows of a late winter storm cut visibility to an arm's length. In the distance, the sound of huge waves breaking over shoal and beach—a sound terrifying to a seaman's ear—could be heard.

Aboard the *Mermaid,* transport ship of the Crown, bound from Halifax to New York with troops for the American Revolution, the Master barked orders to the helm, and to the men high in the rigging trimming sails, hidden from view by snow and stinging spray. It was March 31, 1779, the ship and its crew were fighting for their lives, driven far off course by the elements.

No friendly beacon appeared to warn the vessel of the direction or proximity of the fatal shoreline at Egg Harbor, or the treacherous reefs but a mile offshore, and at 5 A.M. the ship crashed on the shore, its masts and rigging collapsing, and vicious waves sweeping its decks, washing men to their doom.

Thirty-one hours later, rescuers managed to reach the remains of the stranded wreck and save forty-two persons clinging to debris. Dead or missing were one hundred and forty-five soldiers and crewmen . . . history does not relate the number that eventually succumbed to the effects of frozen limbs and shock.

The *Mermaid* was not the first vessel to perish along the Jersey coast, nor would it be the last. But it was very typical of the hundreds of craft to meet a similar fate along a coastline infamous for its dearth of navigational signals. The Egg Harbors area—Brigantine and Absecon beaches—could grimly boast more than its share of ship disasters.

Dr. Jonathan Pitney, who one day would be called the "Father of Atlantic City," was acutely aware of the dangers to seafarers existing along the sand beaches he had come to regard as so beneficial otherwise to human health. In the mid-1830's Pitney, who had arrived in Absecon by horseback, a dusty stranger to South Jersey only fifteen years earlier, started fighting for a maritime beacon, a lighthouse, to warn ships unwarily close to the coast of danger.

For twenty years Jonathan Pitney battled to save lives. His letters and pleas to the federal government fell upon deaf ears. The schooners *Louisa, Ann, Nile, Duroc;* ships *George Cannon, Frankfort* and *Gherge's Kahn;* and scores of others, closed their logbooks between Great and Little Egg Harbor.

Why the government opposed construction of a lighthouse in an area so frequently the scene of water-borne tragedy is a moot question. Carnesworthe, in his 1868 *History of Atlantic City* states Pitney *"had to fight prejudice, and especially prejudice against improvements, that at that time reigned supreme among the 'grannies' of the Navy Department."* Apparently, even eleven years after the lighthouse was approved and operating, there was a trace of bitterness over the battle necessary to establish the lighthouse.

Early in the 1840's, however, the Navy Department received instructions to make a study at Absecon Beach to determine the need, or lack of it, for a lighthouse. Congress appropriated five thousand dollars on the condition that a satisfactory report be received, a token gesture probably designed to placate the crusading South Jersey Doctor, Jonathan Pitney.

One of the most disastrous shipwrecks occurred April 16, 1854, when the ship *Powhatan* carrying three hundred and eleven emigrants plus crew beached two miles above Little Egg Harbor, with no survivors. This would have been within warning view of Absecon Light, had it existed, with the possibility the ship could have avoided disaster. Space does not permit a full listing of known shipwrecks that have occurred before the commissioning, and within warning range, of the Absecon Lighthouse.

Commodore La Vallette, instructed to investigate and report on the feasibility of the project, examined the coast and voluminous records prepared by Pitney, and turned thumbs down on the lighthouse. The project then slept for several years. Between 1847 and 1856 at least sixty-four more ocean-going craft foundered on Absecon Beach . . . more were lost to the north and south along the coast.

Pitney again agitated for what had easily become his pet project. He wrote Congressmen, gathered petitions, and published articles. Finally, in 1856 his efforts clicked. Congress gave in, convinced by Pitney and the increasing reports of shipping losses, as coastal trade increased. Thirty-five thousand dollars was appropriated, and the foundation for the "Absecom Lighthouse" was laid in the sand dunes at the water's edge.

The job proceeded without a hitch, and finally, on Thursday, January 15, 1857, the "Funck's" mineral oil lamp was fired, and a brilliant fixed white light, concentrated and intensified by a "Fresnel lens of the first order," stabbed the darkness over Absecon Beach. Visible nineteen to twenty miles at sea in a direction from N.E. by N. around eastward to S.W., the beacon vastly lessened the threat to ships that, as early as 1695, gave Absecon Beach the nickname "Graveyard Inlet." Dr. Pitney had won his fight.

The Absecon Lighthouse is 167 feet high, placing the beam higher above sea level than any other light on the Jersey coast, except the Twin Highland's Lights. A spiral iron stair of 228 steps leads to the platform at the base of the light fixture, with 12 more steps to the light room. Its base diameter is 26 feet, 4 inches and tapers to 12 feet at the top. Its inside diameter, top to bottom, is 10 feet, making the wall thickness at the base 8 feet 2 inches.

During the years the light was oil powered, it used two gallons of fuel during the summer and three and a half gallons during the winter, when nights are longer. A total of 598,634 bricks were used in its construction.

It remained unpainted until August 14, 1871, when three fifty-foot wide bands, white, red, and white, were applied. More brilliant colors of orange, black, and orange were used when the structure was repainted in August of 1897, and these remained until the present colors of white, blue, and white were used in the repainting of the lighthouse in 1948.

The mineral oil lamps gave way to incandescent oil vapor lamps on the 22nd of June, 1910, and were used until the installation of electric power on Wednesday, July 1, 1925.

Frank Butler's *Book of the Boardwalk* lists several keepers of the light, including Joseph Bartlett, John Nixon, Abram Wolf, Thomas Bills — 1897 — and Knud Hanson in 1915. The light has been known variously as "Absecum,"

"Absecom," "Absekom," and finally Absecon Light, "Absecom" being recorded officially at an early date.

The Absecon Light, located officially in Latitude 39° 21′ 56″, and Longitude 74° 24′ and 53″, cost a total of $52,187 by the date of commissioning, a small fraction, indeed, of the value of maritime losses recorded prior to the initial lighting of the lamp.

In the years to follow, the value of the Absecon Light, and the accuracy of Dr. Pitney's reasoning in spite of Navy Department opposition, was proven scores of times. The light was a deterrent to naval tragedy, and, although there were shipwrecks between Great Egg Harbor and Little Egg Harbor in the years the Absecon Light operated, their frequency and magnitude were greatly decreased. The ships and schooners *C. F. Young, Clara Davidson* and *Amelia* were among those that found their final port near the sands of Absecon Beach despite the friendly beacon at Atlantic City.

As years passed and the twentieth century progressed, the value of the light diminished. Where once no building on Absecon Island was above four floors high, one was built above the hundred-foot mark in 1890, and in two decades buildings were being built even higher than the lighthouse. Mariners complained it was invisible from some points out to sea, obscured by buildings. Finally, a new light, atop a steel tower seventy feet high, was erected along the Boardwalk at New Hampshire Avenue and on Friday, June 9, 1933, was lighted.

The venerable Absecon Light was useless, and was decommissioned on Tuesday, July 11, 1933. No record will ever show the number of vessels that owe their life to the old light at Atlantic City, the product of a rural doctor's dream.

The Light again found itself in headlines, when, in 1946, public sentiment saved the structure from the wrecker's sledge, and on August 10 of that year, the federal government deeded the structure to the city. Not so fortunate were two fine buildings at the light's base, used for years by the Coast Guard as a lifesaving station. Although the buildings would have made superb marine museums, they were demolished.

Today, the Absecon Lighthouse, once at the very water's edge, stands at Rhode Island and Pacific avenues, in Atlantic City, the ocean having receded some two blocks. It is seldom visited, and totally closed to the public. The light, and the park that surrounds it, are in sore need of care and attention.

The lighthouse is in visually sound condition. There are no apparent cracks in the massive walls, and the iron stair that winds to the top shows little or no rusting. Its fastenings are probably as secure as the day they were installed. Rest platforms are found about every three dozen steps. In the light room, the original Fresnel lens is in near perfect condition. The view from the lookout platform beggars description.

Closed to the public, of no maritime value, the light is almost a liability, were it not for its tremendous historic significance. It could be a huge asset to the World's Playground, an attraction for visitors, and an educational, interpretive device, should its door be opened once again to the general public. Public sentiment, aroused by the coming Jersey Tercentenary Year, may again demand this, once again rescuing Absecon Island's guardian of the coast.

Monument at Columbus Plaza, on North Arkansas Avenue, to events in Atlantic City's development

Believed to be Home of John Leeds, Early Resident of Absecon Island, located on North Leeds Place near Arctic Avenue

Atlantic City-Absecon Island

Old Turnpike, first road over salt marshes to Atlantic City, opened in 1870

Monument honoring Jeremiah Leeds, first white settler on Absecon Island, located at Park Place and the Boardwalk.

Lucy, The Elephant

Located on the Beach in Margate at Cedar Grove Avenue.

AN ELEPHANT that never saw a circus, has never touched a peanut, and never even lived, has provided countless thousands of visitors to the Atlantic City area more enjoyment, perhaps, than any of her more animate relatives. Her home is on the Margate sands, and her sightless eyes have been scanning the pounding surf and distant horizon for more than seventy-five years.

The giant pachyderm—and she is indeed a giant—is the Margate Elephant at Cedar Grove Avenue on the beach, and her name is "Lucy."

Lucy was built for a James V. Lafferty, designer of several buildings resembling animals. Although Lucy originally had two "sisters," one at Coney Island and the other at Cape May, they disappeared by 1896, the former by fire, and the other torn down. The Margate Elephant is the lone survivor of a strange breed.

Historians differ regarding Lucy's origin. Some accounts state she was built in Margate with a live elephant as a model, and constructed to scale. Another story tells of her being erected for an exhibit at the Philadelphia Centennial Exhibition in 1876, and then transported to Margate.

The elephant was used in the early 1900's for a hotel and tavern. Phil Rohr, an early bartender, is said to have installed electric lights because tipsy patrons had a habit of upsetting oil lamps and nearly causing fires.

A severe storm and flooding brought Lucy to her tin knees in 1903, when the swirling waters undermined her front feet and she sank to her kneecaps in the sand. A house mover, Rufus Booye, raised her to her former, more dignified height, and placed her some fifty feet back from the original location.

The howdah on Lucy's back is sixty-five feet above ground, and contains an observation platform. Her eyes are windows measuring eighteen inches in diameter. The rooms inside her eighty-foot long body are reached by spiral stairs up one of the huge legs.

Today, Lucy still remains an outstanding and unusual attraction for many history buffs and visitors alike, and a unique sidelight to South Jersey's history.

NOTE: *Although events and structures occurring after 1875 have been excluded from this book, the Margate Elephant was considered sufficiently unusual to be the exception to the rule.*

The Old Customs House

*Located on Shore Road, Linwood, attached to the rear of
the private residence of Mr. & Mrs. Harold Appleyard at
#1444 Shore Road. (Not open to public)*

SOMERS POINT was the old port of entry for Gloucester County, and as such a customs house was established in 1791 in Leedsville (Linwood), with Daniel Benezet, Jr. appointed Collector of Customs on March 21 of that year.

Vessels arriving in the territory under the charge of the Customs District of Great Egg Harbor were obliged to register here, pay whatever duties were levied, and, at times, have cargoes inspected, before proceeding to their destinations. Goods salvaged from the many shipwrecks occurring along the South Jersey coast were also normally recorded here.

A complete list of Collectors of Customs for the district includes:

Daniel Benezet, Jr.	March 21, 1791
Constant Somers	February 25, 1795
Alexander Freeland	August 16, 1799
Joseph Winner	March 26, 1804
Matthew Collins	March 24, 1809
Jesse Somers	November 8, 1809
Ezra Baker	February 18, 1813
Gideon Leeds	March 2, 1815
Mahlon D. Canfield	January 14, 1830
Richard C. Holmes	March 20, 1849
Thomas D. Winner	March 19, 1853
Israel S. Adams	May 31, 1861
John Price	January 12, 1885
James Tilton	October 20, 1885
John Price	January 15, 1890
Enoch A. Higbee	February 5, 1894
Walter Fifield	February 11, 1903
Lewis R. Barrett	August 24, 1912

The original commission of Jesse Somers, appointing him "Collector of Customs for the District of Great Egg Harbor," and signed by James Madison, President of the United States at the time, is in the possession of the Atlantic County Historical Society.

Gideon Leeds, Collector, offered for sale in 1827, *"94 packages of goods saved out of the Schooner Dart,"* wrecked in Great Egg Harbor.

Port activities had all but ceased when, in 1913, the Bureau of Customs was reorganized by authority of a Presidential message to Congress, dated March 3 of that year. Under this reorganization the Customs District of Great Egg Harbor was discontinued and Somers Point, the port of entry, became a subport in the Customs District of Philadelphia.*

The old customs house has been converted to living quarters in the rear of a fine home built along Shore Road in 1853. The house itself, built by Thomas Morris, Deputy Collector, is worthy of note, because it follows the typical Down Jersey lines of architecture used during that era throughout South Jersey. Because of its excellent condition it is an outstanding example of early Atlantic County residences.

* Letter from W. Neil Franklin, Acting Chief, Diplomatic, Legal and Fiscal Branch, B of C. U.S.T.D.

Mid-nineteenth-century Jersey residence in Linwood. Early Great Egg Harbor District Customs House attached to rear of house and not visible from the road.

Jeremiah Leeds, Pioneer

Grave located center of Oxford Circle, Northfield.

SAND DUNES, nearly eight miles of them, broken only by an occasional creek and dotted with bayberry and small pine forests, formed an island primeval, populated solely by shore and song birds which left glistening beaches only to soar in easy quest of food.

This was the scene to greet Jeremiah Leeds about 1783, when he first set foot on Absecon Island, a land sighted and recorded by Henry Hudson in 1609, and purchased for four cents an acre in 1685 by Thomas Budd.

Leeds, a Jerseyman born at Leeds Point, March 4, 1754, had married one Judith Steelman in 1776. It was her father, Frederick Steelman, who in later years, purchased much of Absecon Island, and property in Northfield.

A private, and later a lieutenant in the New Jersey Militia during the Revolutionary War, Jeremiah Leeds had been stationed in brief hitches throughout South Jersey, and during service in Colonel Richard Somers' regiment had found himself in the thick of the fray at Chestnut Neck.

The pioneer couple—the first perma-

nent settlers — cleared a section of high land and cultivated the soil. Sailing vessels plying the coast paused to secure fresh produce from the island farmer. In time, Leeds expanded and raised horses, cattle, and sheep, and the island became known as "Leeds' Beach."

Effort brought prosperity, and the "plantation" soon included a log cabin boasting two rooms and a huge fireplace that formed one wall of the kitchen. But in time this was replaced by a more comfortable frame dwelling where the family lived except for periods during the birth of Leeds' ten children, only one of whom was born on Absecon Island.

Jeremiah Leeds remarried after the death of Judith. His second wife, Millicent, was the mother of four of his ten children.

Absecon Island's first citizen and resident died October 10, 1838, at the age of eighty-four years, and was buried in Northfield. Little could he have known that scores of new settlers, already taking up residence on the island, would in sixteen short years petition the Secretary of State in Trenton for incorporation papers creating from a tiny village a town they would call Atlantic City.

Risley Homestead

Residence of Mr. & Mrs. Howard Stout, 8 Virginia Avenue, Northfield.

AMONG THE EARLY settlers in Gloucester County were the Risleys. The old homestead in Northfield is believed to have been built during the late eighteenth century on the family farm, which at the time was about a mile square.

Foundations are of Jersey stone, and many original glass panes remain in the windows. Framing in the building is peg fastened, and stone mortar was made of oyster shells, as was common in early Jersey.

The old fireplace, crane, and paneling remain to this day in the living room of the homestead.

The residence of Dr. Jonathan Pitney, in Absecon. The original section
(left) is believed to have been built prior to 1800. The larger
portion was constructed in the 1860's.

Dr. Pitney's House

Situated on southwest corner Shore Road and Church Street in Absecon.

SADDLEBAGS packed with medical supplies, and some clothing, a blanket, and strong cloth rolled behind his saddle, a young man rode into town.

The village was Absecum (Absecon), the year was about 1819, and the horseman was young Dr. Jonathan Pitney. Only twenty-two years old, Pitney had just completed two years as an assistant in a hospital at Staten Island, following his graduation from New York medical schools.

Probably few noticed the youthful horseman as he arrived in the village. Certainly no one knew or cared that he had just completed the long saddle trip from his birthplace and home in Mendham, Morris County, where he had been born October 29, 1797. How could anyone have foreseen that this young doctor would become forever famous, to be called one day the "Father of Atlantic City," Queen Resort of the Coast. He was to be responsible for the construction of the railroad east across Jersey and the salt marshes to Absecum Island.

His efforts were to cause the federal government to construct and commission a lighthouse at the north end of Absecum Island, finally putting an end to the countless scores of shipwrecks occurring on the shoals and beaches near "Graveyard Inlet."

Dr. Pitney settled on Kings Highway in Absecum, a road known today as the "Shore Road." (Although Shore Road has been rerouted at many points, several remaining sections, such as in Higbeetown near Smithville, still bear the name Kings Highway.)

Miss Caroline Fowler, of Absecum, became the bride of the physician in 1831.

Their residence was the Fowler home along Kings Highway.

Jonathan Pitney, the citizen, was prominent in public life. When Gloucester County divided and its eastern portion became the County of Atlantic, Pitney was on hand to participate actively in the negotiations.

In 1844 he became a delegate to Trenton, to the convention drafting the revised Constitution of New Jersey.

But it was his interest in his fellow man that led to the founding of the World's Playground. Pitney would frequently be found along the beaches of Absecum Island, walking, exercising, swimming. His errands of mercy to the island to minister to the needs of the scattered settlers were invariably concluded with relaxing moments at the shore.

The island still had only a handful of residents when Dr. Pitney started fighting for a railroad to be built to the shore. He realized that with transportation other than that of the rough-riding stagecoaches, the island would grow, and increasing numbers of people, residents and visitors alike, would be able to enjoy the healthful atmosphere of the coast.

Atlantic City was incorporated March 3, 1854. By July 4 of that year, passenger traffic began on the Camden and Atlantic Railroad, and the city began to grow.

Dr. Jonathan Pitney died at the age of seventy-two, on August 7, 1869. He had literally built Atlantic City, a railroad, and a lighthouse, and had been able to watch his wildest dreams materialize. He had earned his nickname, "The Father of Atlantic City."

The Clark's Grave

Found on a wooded island, end of Clarks Landing Road, 15 minutes walk west of road terminus, overlooking Mullica River.

CLARK'S LANDING was one of the very earliest settlements in old Gloucester County. It was founded on the south shore of the Little Egg Harbor River, about ten miles inland, early in the eighteenth century.

The Landing, by 1718, was a thriving community, with a log church, general store, some forty houses mostly of log construction, a storehouse, and a population of more than two hundred and seventy-five souls. Nearly two decades later, the log homes had been largely replaced by frame dwellings of native Jersey cedar, the church had been rebuilt, and a spacious frame building doubled as a store, town hall, and trading post. The population had increased to more than four hundred residents.

Two early settlers at the Landing were Thomas and Ruth Clark. Virtually nothing is known of their lives or of much of the development and decline of the village. The final resting place of the two Clarks is all that remains today of Clark's Landing, a once flourishing settlement.

Their graves are a fifteen-minute trek through dense pines, briars, and rhododendron, and accessible only after the careful crossing of a tiny creek and swamp marsh. They are still legible: *"Here Lyes . . . Thomas Clark . . . died 1752 . . . Here Lyes . . . Mrs. Ruth Clark . . . died 1745."*

Only the shovel and trowel of the archaeologist, using care and skill in slow and tedious excavation, can read of the eighteenth-century existence of this pioneer community.

Wanton vandalism recently occurred at Clark's Landing. The headstones of the Clarks had been set in cement about thirty years ago to preserve the markers and their delicate inscriptions. The footstones had been allowed to stand, although set firmly in the cement.

When visited by the writer about two years ago, these footstones were still in place, although covered with leaves and briars. During a visit a year ago, it was found that the two footstones had been deliberately broken and removed. That the public had no more respect for graves of any age, not to mention their historical heritage, is both inconceivable and unfortunate. It is regrettable that New Jersey does not have an Antiquities Act that would tend to discourage the criminal vandalism of the State's historical areas and artifacts.

(top) Grave markers of Thomas (1752) and Ruth (1745) Clark at Clark's Landing. The inscriptions have been chalked making them legible to the camera.
The Clarks' Graves as they appeared in 1961, showing Jersey stone footstones in place (bottom left)
Same graves in 1962, showing the cement slab holding the headstones, but with the footstones removed by vandals (bottom right)

Here Lyes the Body of MR THOMAS CLARK who Died 17 A.D. 1752 In the 63 Year of His Age

Here Lyes y Body of Mrs Ruth Clark Wife of Mr Thos Clark who Died Jan Year of Her

Legend of the Jersey Devil

SHEDDING AN EERIE, wavering, yellow glow about the room, the solitary candle flickered, as traces of wintery winds filtered through the cabin walls and about the ill-fitted windows and doors. Only the cheerful glow of a roaring fire in the hearth lent a cozy, homey atmosphere to the austere appearance of the farmhouse kitchen.

Upstairs, in the tiny rooms of the structure, slept a dozen children, ranging in age to their late teens. It was the early eighteenth century and the setting was a backwoods farm in Leeds Point, along the eastern extremity of old Gloucester County, deep in Southern Jersey.

Mother Leeds was a middle-aged woman, but the effects wrought by the rigors of an early colonist's life and the bearing of many children made her appear far older. She sat, hunched over the table, glaring at the candle's flame, unmindful of the boiling pot suspended in the huge old cooking fireplace.

Suspected by her neighbors of being a witch and sorceress, Mother Leeds looked the part. Her unkempt appearance when visiting in the village only added to the rumors.

Today, she had discovered she was to give birth to another—a thirteenth—child. And she cursed upon the announcement: "I shall never bring a thirteenth child into the world," she had screamed, "and if I do, upon my oath, it shall be a monster, a devil."

The months passed, and the vigorous South Jersey winter turned to spring and then to summer. Finally, Mother Leeds gave birth to her child, and when she saw it she unleashed a piercing scream, while those in attendance stood back horrified.

Mother Leeds's curse upon her thirteenth child had apparently come true.

For he was indeed a creature, a human boy to be sure, but horribly deformed and ugly as . . . the Devil himself.

Very soon after the creature was born, Mother Leeds carried it into the lightless cellar, and fashioning a cradle and lining it with straw, laid the young boy in place. Regularly, she came to feed her offspring, and in time she actually seemed pleased that her curse had come true.

The years passed, and Mother Leeds continued to care for her horribly deformed and now mentally deficient child. Occasionally whispers of fear and protest would circulate through the neighborhood, but invariably people would allow them to die down of their own accord.

Then it happened — Mother Leeds became gravely ill. Since she could not care for the creature hidden for so many years in the cellar, it escaped one night. Neighbors from the surrounding countryside investigated one morning to find the cause of uproars in their barnyards the night before.

They came to Mother Leeds's house, and discovered the heavy oaken doors leading to her cellar splintered apart. The creature they knew had been harbored in the darkness below was gone.

They rushed into the house to find Mother Leeds on her deathbed, and unattended.

Now coastal South Jersey, in the mid-eighteenth-century was a sparsely populated rural area, with dense and vast cedar swamps and marshlands. Although a quarry could elude pursuers indefinitely with very little effort, the villagers formed posses to trace Mrs. Leeds's devil-son. But he was not found. Instead, from time to time, farmers would awaken to tend to their chores and find cattle slaughtered and torn apart by some incredible animal-like creature.

These occurrences, of course, were blamed on Mrs. Leeds's devil-son, and as the years progressed, although the incidents stopped, the legend persisted.

Every time a farmer's field of wheat failed to ripen, it was because the Leeds Devil had passed, or when a cow's milk soured, it was because the Leeds Devil had touched the animal. The strange creature born to Mother Leeds was never found. The actual instances involving raids on farmers' flocks and herds ceased to occur, but legend and folklore being what it is, every time a mysterious or unexplained incident happens, every time a strange series of footprints are found in the sands along the Mullica River, every time a strange shape is seen in the height of a Down Jersey thunderstorm, the blame is attached to the Leeds Devil, known now as the Jersey Devil.

The story of the Jersey Devil has been reconstructed from the folklore and writings about him that have appeared over the years. There can be no doubt that the creature was born to Mrs. Leeds, that he did grow to maturity, that he did escape, and did raid farmers' yards and livestock. There is also little doubt that he was never found, but in this day and age, we can rest safe in the knowledge, that however inhuman the creature appeared he ultimately met his fate. That folklore persisted is the very nature of folklore. Rest safe, dear reader, that the Jersey Devil is no more, or is he?

Industries of the County

FISHING, clamming, and farming have changed little in the two hundred and fifty-odd years they have been a main livelihood for South Jerseymen. Boats still leave their berths in the harbors and bays for the deeper sea, to cast and haul their nets or "jig" for fish. Clammers still wade in shallow waters of the bay, treading for clams with bare feet and retrieving them by hand or even by foot. Even "catching" clams with "tongs," long wooden scissorlike poles with metaltined "hands" at the end, dates to a century and a half ago.

Farmers have swapped the horse and ox for a motor-powered tractor, but their crops are still a product of the soil, and much harvesting is done by hand labor. Atlantic County is still famous for its earliest industries, and its products are shipped world-wide.

Tobacco was a major crop during the eighteenth century, and many were the colonial clay pipes that were filled with the leaf from Jersey. So important was tobacco farming that even the shilling bank note currency of that era was imprinted with a tobacco leaf on the reverse side.

But as the years progressed, new industry came into the picture. By the turn of the nineteenth century, iron furnaces and forges had been built and were turning out products not only for the Revolutionary War, but for households throughout the colonies. Their iron was smelted from bog ore, a variety of limonite, mined in the swamps near the furnaces. The hearths were fired with wood, usually made into charcoal first, cut from the vast forests that surrounded the furnaces, and each furnace owned or had rights to as much as twenty-five thousand acres of timber in the neighborhood.

A record noted in 1832 for Gloucester County shows 102 stores, 21 fisheries,

45 grist mills, 2 cotton and 2 woolen factories, 4 carding machines, 4 blast furnaces, 3 forges, 63 saw mills, 4 fulling mills, 8 ferries, 9 tanning yards, 29 distilleries, and 7 glass factories in existence, most of which were located in what would five years later become Atlantic County.

A castor oil factory was operated at Leeds Point betwen 1822 and 1824 by Japhet, Samuel, and Barzillai Leeds, Timothy Pharo, and Daniel Smith. They grew castor oil beans in surrounding fields, cooked the oil, and shipped it to Philadelphia and New York outlets.

The making of wine and the growing of grapes for wine started locally about the mid-nineteenth-century, and Atlantic County still boasts many wineries producing some of the nation's finest wines. These are still located at Egg Harbor, Absecon, and Hammonton and elsewhere.

Glassmaking began as the iron furnaces gradually ceased operations. The discovery of coal in Pennsylvania marked the death knell for Jersey's furnaces, and many of the iron makers turned to glass. Crowleytown Glassworks, across the Mullica from Atlantic County and about four miles from Batsto, is credited with producing the very first Mason jar in 1858. Window and bottle glass was turned out at Estellville Glassworks as early as 1826.

Fine cut glass was produced in the Egg Harbor area late in the nineteenth century and well into the 1930's. The art has been revived in this area recently.

Cotton was produced at Pleasant Mills, and the paper mills at Pleasant Mills and Weymouth operated for many years.

But it was not until 1854, and through the efforts of Dr. Jonathan Pitney, that Atlantic County founded its most outstanding industry—an industry that overshadows all others because it provides not only income for the county's people but health and pleasure for mankind.

Sandwiched between the great population centers of America, New York and Philadelphia, and with more than one third of the population of the United States within two hours' travel by modern automobile, the seashore resort industry has proven most beneficial.

Refreshing salt air, strong sunlight unobscured by industrial smoke, and facilities unexcelled for health and pleasure have made Atlantic County's biggest industry, now more than a century old, its greatest asset.

Fishing is Atlantic County's earliest industry, dating from more than 250 years ago, to a period when settlements in this area were but a handful of fishing hamlets dotting the mainland coast, at the headwaters of streams and the edge of the rivers. Photographs on the next two pages show the South Jersey menhaden or "bunker" fleet, moored at the docks in Atlantic City.
(pages 106–7)

Estellville Glass Works

Ruins found in woodland, 0.4 miles from Route 50,
accessible by permission of South River Game Farm.

STEPHEN'S CREEK flows through the cedar swamps and pinelands to empty its rich brown "cedar water" into the Great Egg Harbor River. The woodlands along its shores are dense now, inhabited principally by wild game and waterfowl. Only sportsmen visit the winding woods roads and trails, and there is little intimation of the thriving community that once existed there.

This is Estellville, now part of Estell Manor, a quiet, rural South Jersey community that once boasted a vast glassworks and an iron forge, and claims, along with Leeds Point, the dubious distinction of having been the birthplace of the Jersey Devil.

Stephen's Creek was described in 1834 as a *"village and post town containing a grist mill, saw mill, tavern, store, and six or eight dwellings."* Situated alongside the Estellville Glassworks, the hamlet served the employees at the works, a scant mile distant.

John H. Scott built the Estellville Works in 1825. Here, in the bog ore and mud furnaces were made window glass and bottle glass, the workmen toiling from sunrise to sunset.

In 1834 Scott, who had operated the works alone, sold his business to Daniel Estell, a founder of Estelleville, or, as it is now known, Estellville. Several years passed and a brother of Daniel, John, and a brother-in-law, Josiah Franklin, bought an interest in the industry.

By 1844, the Estellville Glassworks employed eighty men. While workers would concentrate on the window and bottle glass, it is known that their spare time at the end of the day was frequently devoted to turning out craft items of glass, enabling them to maintain and develop their skill at blowing and molding glass. These items may have included ornate glass canes, pitchers, beads, vases, and even paperweights.

A *section of brick wall, showing two arches, part of the glassworks ruins*

Much *of the Estellville Works was constructed of Jersey stone—bog ore. Although the mortar is crumbling, much of the stone is still firmly in place.*

The old glassworks still remain in Estellville. But no longer do the furnaces turn out glass. The fires are stilled forever, and the walls of the vast works are crumbling to the ravages of time and the elements.

Workers' houses nearby are decaying too, no longer resounding to the activities of early family life in Gloucester County. Vandals have looted the ruins of everything of value. The Estellville Glassworks are a fading monument to a colorful region and era in our local history. Through neglect, the area is following many other Atlantic County historic sites into oblivion.

A section of the extensive ruins of the Estellville Glassworks ⟩

⟨ *All that remains today of one of the typical worker's houses; the walls have fallen and only a tall twin fireplace chimney still stands.*

How Glass Was Made

FURNACE ROOMS for nineteenth-century glassworks in South Jersey and Atlantic County were large, the operation involving white-hot glass demanding an earthen floor. The extreme temperatures of the furnace chambers, ranging at times as high as 2,600 degrees Fahrenheit, dictated a very high-ceilinged room.

The furnace proper, which generally was in the center of the room, was usually oblong, although many square furnaces have been found. They included a melting or combustion chamber and an area called the ash pit or "cave." The areas were separated by a raised platform called a "siege" upon which crucibles containing ingredients of glass were placed.

Extending the full length of the furnace, the ash pit provided an air draft. Along the sides of the furnace were small holes through which the crucibles could be charged. Flames in the combustion chamber were directed at the crucibles for periods up to thirty or forty hours, which was required for the melting process to produce glass "metal."

When the metal was in readiness it was white hot and in a fluid state. It had to be cooled to a brilliant red heat before it could be used by the blowers.

The glass blower took his blowpipe, a tapering hollow tube some four to seven feet in length, and placed the "nose" of the pipe in the crucible of molten glass, accumulating a quantity of the metal on the end. He would then turn and roll the gathered material on a polished metal plate until it was uniform in size.

The glass was then blown by puffing air through the blowpipe carefully, until the gathered metal reached the desired expanded size. The pipe could be rolled or swung to change the shape of the glass piece. The glass would be much cooler now, but could still be shaped if necessary with a metal bar or rod.

A solid iron bar called a "puntee" or "puntil" rod, usually shorter than the blowpipe, was then attached to the end of the glass piece directly opposite to the blowpipe, a piece of tacky glass joining the two. An assistant, called a "wetter-off," would then detach the blowpipe by touching the neck of the glass item with a wet piece of iron and tapping the glass. The opening that remained could then be shaped further with a bar or rod of iron, and flanged, cut, or otherwise fashioned with a spout by the "chairman," who rolled the glass piece, still fastened to the end of the puntee, back and forth on the arm of his chair.

Oftentimes, the mouth of the glass piece had to be slightly reheated, so the shaping and forming operations could be completed. The puntee bar was then detached with a sharp blow, but not until a handle, if desired, was attached. This was done simply by applying one end of hot and still pliable glass to the glass item in production, and stretching it as desired, finally looping it to the top or bottom of the piece, creating a handle.

Finally, the glass piece was carried on a forked stick to the annealing oven. It was placed inside, and, under delicately controlled heat, the glass would be tempered. lest it crack and break at the slightest jar. In late years (till about 1860) glass items were annealed by placing the piece on an iron "leer-pan." This was then placed on a small iron wagon, which was run slowly through the annealing oven.

When this was accomplished, the glassware piece was finished. It could be further decorated by etching, or cutting with abrasive wheels.

The production of glass was and is still a major industry in South Jersey, and especially the Atlantic County area, and glasswares produced in South Jersey, from the days of the first Jersey glassworks at Wistarberg, Salem County, one of the earliest in America, are now among the most valuable of collectors' treasures.

Gloucester Furnace

Site on west side of Bremen Avenue, 1.0 miles south of Gloucester (Clarks Landing) Road, Egg Harbor City vicinity.

GLOUCESTER was another of the early Jersey iron furnaces owned by the Richards family, one of a chain that included Batsto, Weymouth, and Atsion furnaces. The village that surrounded it was a post town, and located on Landing Creek, a tributary of the Mullica River.

Fires at old Gloucester were first lit in 1785–86. Records show that in 1785 William Richards owned fifteen hundred acres of property in Galloway Township,

with *"a mill and a forge thereon."* The Gloucester Furnace lands abutted those of Batsto Furnace some seven miles to the northwestward.

Many accounts heretofore published claim Gloucester was not built until 1813. The tax lists for Galloway Township clearly disprove this, marking the furnace as colonial eighteenth century, existing in 1785.

George Richards, with his brother Mark and Benjamin Jones, acquired

Gloucester Furnace in 1825, reselling it in 1830 to Thomas Richards, a merchant of Philadelphia, and his cousin, John Richards of Gloucester County. Some years later, Stephen Colwell of Weymouth acquired the land and furnace.

In 1830 the Gloucester Furnace property consisted of a charcoal blast furnace, a saw mill, tenant houses, and sixteen to seventeen thousand acres of land. A grist mill on Landing Creek was erected about this time, and a tavern added by 1834. By that year, eight thousand more acres of land were added to the holdings.

The furnace capacity was about twenty-five tons of iron weekly, from which stoves, lamp posts, and special castings were made. Some of the stoves were the celebrated stoves invented by Dr. Nott of Albany, New York, noted during that era for iron design.

A fine brick ironmaster's mansion overlooked the lake feeding Landing Creek, built by George Richards.

But by 1855 Gloucester was on the decline. Competition with furnaces in Pennsylvania had doomed the Jersey iron villages, which relied on wood, rather than on the more plentiful and easily obtainable coal, and a low grade of iron ore. In that year the fires were extinguished for the last time, and the lands sold to Stephen Colwell, who in turn sold to Dr. Henry Schmole of Philadelphia, organizer of the Gloucester Land and Town Association, parent settlement of Egg Harbor City.

Of Gloucester Furnace, nothing remains today. The stack, buildings, houses, tavern, all are vanished. Only deposits of slag and pieces of iron can be found on the shores of Landing Creek. Even current and old maps erroneously place the furnace location on the north side of Gloucester (Clarks Landing) Road near the Mullica River.

There was a settlement there, and old cellar foundations can still easily be found. But this was Gloucester Landing, and was easily a mile from the main village of Gloucester. But Nature is healing her wounds, and a growing forest now stands where once iron was made from bog ore.

Etna Furnace

Site on north side of Tuckahoe River, south side of Head of River Road, one mile from Route 49 (east) and four miles west of Tuckahoe.

ETNA FURNACE was opened between 1815 and 1817, and a forge connected with the works mentioned in a deed dated December 27, 1816, was located some two miles distant. It probably operated under the management of Joshua Howell and John R. Coates. The only positive management known was John Ladd Howell, about 1821.

The furnace is known to have made bar iron, spikes, and bolts, and obtained power for the air bellows from water wheels fed by a raceway from the dammed Tuckahoe River. Charging the furnace was accomplished by wheeling ore, charcoal, and flux up an inclined ramp to the opening at the top.

Of Etna, only a crumbled pile of brick remains, and this is secreted under accumulations of leaves and brush. Another bit of Old Jersey has vanished.

Iron Furnace at Weymouth

Furnace ruins located along the Great Egg Harbor River, in Weymouth, 0.4 miles north of Black Horse Pike, on easterly side of secondary road to Hammonton.

REMOTE AND PICTURESQUE, the Great Egg Harbor River flows through the cedar swamps, pine, and oak woods past the near-ghost village of Weymouth. Here, the waters describe a horseshoe curve, and nearly surround all that today remains of one of South Jersey's busiest iron furnaces.

A tall brick chimney towers some sixty feet above crumbling Jersey stone walls. Stone arches still span tiny sluicelike creeks, branching from the main river. A mineral spring that offered a healthful but odorous drink to the visitor only half a dozen years ago is marked only by the stone tub it once filled.

A bar of pig iron, cast of Jersey bog ore at Weymouth, early in the 1800's. Ironworkers nicknamed this a pig, the molten iron in its sand forms resembling suckling pigs.

Vines and weeds scale the fallen walls in an effort to claim the furnace's remains and hide them from view. It is difficult to picture the furnace as the beehive of activity it presented during the early nineteenth century.

An early gazetteer of New Jersey, published in 1834, describes Weymouth: *"—Blast furnace, forge and village, in Hamilton t-ship, Gloucester Co., upon the Great Egg Harbor River, about 5 miles above the head of navigation. The furnace makes about 900 tons of castings annually; the forge having four fires and two hammers, makes about 200 tons of bar iron, immediately from the ore. There are also a grist and saw mill, and buildings for the workmen, of whom 100 are constantly employed about the works."*

Weymouth Furnace was established in 1801 by Charles Shoemaker, George Ashbridge, Morris Robeson, John Paul, and Joseph M. Paul, who purchased the vast tract from the West Jersey Society of Proprietors on November 6, 1800, with a net area of 78,060 acres. By 1802 Ashbridge, acting as manager, was advertising for a *"full set of Forgemen to work a New Forge, now erected and in complete order."*

Using native Jersey bog ore, the workers at Weymouth procceded to turn out a wide variety of iron products; stoves, plates, iron pipe, mortars and pestles, were just a few of the many items.

The iron ore was dug from the nearby swamps, and in 1818 a canal was built between the furnace and the "ore ponds." The ore was then loaded on flat-bottom barges and poled to the furnace. Traces of the canal still remain. And even today, in the city of Philadelphia, iron pipe is found that bears the imprint of Weymouth Furnace—a raised W.

Foundations of mill building along an old raceway

There remained along Delaware Avenue in Philadelphia until the 1920's, hitching posts that had been fashioned from old cannon made at Weymouth during the War of 1812, when many articles of warfare were produced.

Excerpts from original record books of the furnace provide an unusual accounting of life and times of the workmen, often taking a humorous twist. Consider the following:

"March 25, 1818	*Aetna furnace Teams past here this evening with loads of goods from Martha Furnace*
June 3, 1818	*Training at Mays Landing. Nearly all came home sober.*
January 2, 1819	*Jacob Hoffman hung himself twice but did not hang Long enough*
October 22, 1819	*Tin Pedler here*
February 10, 1820	*Wm. Richards moved from Atsion to Weymouth today*
February 12, 1820	*. . . killed 64 rabbits*
March 9, 1820	*School commencing this morning*
November 10, 1820	*. . . cool, Doct . . . came to day, S. B. Finch in love with a young lady, he has some notion of making a grab, . . .*
November 29, 1820	*Mr. Richards went coaling . . . throw'd off one coal Box this evening. . . .*

Or this record of production . . .

"May 2, 1819	*Made one Pipe and lost another*
September 21, 1819	*Pipe good this evening*
September 22, 1819	*Made no Pipe A/c of rain*
October 4, 1819	*No Pipes this day bad iron*
October 14, 1819	*Iron good made 2 pipes*
October 23, 1819	*Made no Pipes, iron bad*
October 24, 1819	*Made 2 Pipes"*

Weymouth had attained a special significance when, in 1808, ownership of the tract of land passed to Samuel Richards of Atsion Furnace. This act linked the ironworks closely with the Richards family enterprises, including Atsion and Batsto furnaces, and the account books of the furnaces reveal much trading between them and other South Jersey furnaces.

Samuel Richards died in 1842, and the estate passed to his heirs, including Sarah Ball, wife of Stephen Colwell, Elizabeth and W. Dwight Bell, and Hannah Nicholas. Colwell managed the operation and built a large mansion house overlooking the vast lake that supplied water power for the works. This fine building remained for a century, until the 1950's, when fire claimed it and it burned to the ground.

Weymouth Forge had burned to the ground in 1862, and three years later the furnace suffered the same misfortune.

Stephen Colwell then built a paper mill on the site, and for twenty-one years produced considerable quantities of Manila paper. But in 1887 even this operation ceased and the mill closed permanently.

Mr. Fountain Gale, aged ninety-two and still living at Weymouth in one of the old workers' houses, came to the village after having lived at Clark's Landing, where he was born in 1871. His memories of the Weymouth paper mill are very vivid and accurate, and his stories of playing as a boy among the ruins of Gloucester Furnace, of the stages that traveled the early roads, and of school days in the nineteenth century would fill volumes.

Weymouth Village, the furnace and paper mill ruins, the canal, raceway, and the workers' houses still partially exist. But they are fading into yesteryear. As at other Atlantic County historic areas, the ravages of time and the elements, combined with lack of care, are claiming the ruins.

Fountain Gale, of Weymouth, born at Clark's Landing in 1871, recalls: "The old furnace was gone when we moved here . . . I was 19 years old then . . . but the paper mill was a-goin', and they made lots of fine brown paper . . . the canals were still here, you know they brought the bog ore to the furnace in scows poled on the canals . . . had trouble keepin' an exhaust pipe in my boat. . . . I found a piece of that iron pipe made here at Weymouth, way back, put it in my boat, 'n used it fer years, stuff never rusted, even in salt water. . . . Those were the years, boy, but now, almost nothing left, it's all going. . . ."

But Weymouth is taking a new lease on life. Always a popular retreat for campers, canoeists, and picnickers, it is destined for preservation in its present condition, and steps are being taken to stabilize the ruins to arrest further deterioration.

The Lake Lenape Land Company, recent owners of the Weymouth Furnace Tract, donated the furnace site in December of 1962 to the Atlantic County Historical Society, to be managed until the close of the Tercentennial Year by the Atlantic County Tercentenary Committee.

History buffs and the general public will owe a debt of gratitude to this firm and its ownership, including J. Stanley Tunny of Seaside Heights, Robert Rundle of Pittsburgh, and C. Richard Tunny of Mays Landing.

Weymouth Furnace will never again produce iron, but its preservation will be an exhibit of living history for generations to come.

Weymouth ironworker's home

Raceway after a winter's snow

Outside plumbing for a Weymouth worker's house

Pleasant Mills at Sweetwater

Situated on north side of Weekstown Road (Route 23), 0.2 miles east of Route 542 intersection in Pleasant Mills.

WATER STILL FLOWS through the old mill race, fed by cedar swamps and Lake Nescochague, and past the now crumbling remains of one of the oldest mills in South Jersey.

No longer do the mill wheels turn, and no longer do small vessels drop anchor by the "Pleasant Mills of Sweetwater" to load cotton and thread products. The rich brown "cedar water" is undisturbed now, but for an occasional pickerel breaking surface.

Swamp maples, some oaks, pines, and cedars form a picturesque arch over the waters, and now over the decaying stonework of the vast mill as well. Vines, briers, and falling leaves are reaching out to claim the site that man has almost disowned. Only a small section of the mill has been preserved and reconstructed. It is now a fine private residence, situated in a most romantic setting.

The village was called Sweetwater, when the mill was founded about 1825, because of the excellent quality of the water in the streams. Earlier, it had been called the "Forks," from the time of its founding early in the eighteenth century until after the Revolutionary War.

By 1834 the cotton mill was thriving, its employees handling three thousand spindles. The village had become known as Pleasant Mills, and the name Sweetwater dropped, although the region to the east and just "down the road a piece" is still known by the old name.

It is interesting that this village, just across the Mullica from historic Batsto, boasted a tavern, two stores, a glass factory, twenty to thirty dwellings, and the cotton mill. Today there are still twenty to thirty dwellings and more, but one store and the tavern, as well as both industries, have vanished.

A paper mill replaced the cotton factory about 1861, and except during a rebuilding program following a disastrous fire in 1879, the Pleasant Mills Paper Company operated until the early 1920's.

The paper mill at one time experimented with the production of paper using native South Jersey salt hay, or marsh grass, as the basic ingredient. Some paper was actually turned out, but the operation never became profitable and was discontinued. Another paper mill, located some fourteen miles distant at Harrisville in Burlington County, operating some years earlier, had enjoyed a considerable success before it burned to the ground.

Today, the old mill building is a victim of an apathetic public. Occasional vandals remove bits of iron or stone, and only the section used as a residence is maintained, but that in excellent condition. During recent years, interest was revived in the old site when the Pleasant Mills Players offered stage plays in the nostalgic setting, but now even they, unfortunately, are gone.

The Pleasant Mills of Sweetwater richly deserve preservation. The buildings are part of the story of Batsto, colonial iron village. Without care, they will soon be beyond reasonable restoration, a fate that has befallen many other treasured historic areas.

Affair at Little Egg Harbour

Area on south shore of Mullica River at Chestnut Neck,
8.0 miles north of Absecon on Shore Road, Route 9.

PRIVATEER CAPTAINS found Chestnut Neck, the Mullica River, and the village of the Forks, thirty miles farther inland, well suited to their needs during the days of the American Revolution. This was the area called by Lieutenant General Sir Henry Clinton, Commander in Chief of the British Forces in America, a "nest of rebel pirates," for the exploits here of South Jersey seamen are both legion and legendary.

Headquarters for the privateers was the Forks, far upriver and deep in the Pine Barrens. A scant half mile from the Forks was the colonial iron-making village of Batsto, a principal supplier to George Washington and the Continental Army.

The Mullica River was easily navigable by brigantines, sloops, and similar craft, including the East Indiamen and many merchant and naval vessels seized by the Americans as prizes.

The Forks proved an ideal spot for the final unloading of cargoes carried by prizes and the subsequent sale of both to interested colonists at the highest bid. Cargoes of value to the Continental Army were transported overland for use against the British, for whom they were originally intended.

But the Forks, for vessels of the day, was a full day's sail up the Mullica River, and privateers could ill afford the time consumed by such a journey. Consequently, they looked elsewhere for a place that would serve for the replenishment of food and water stores, as well as for minor repairs to their ships, which were often necessitated by the blowing away of rigging and superstructure as a result of naval engagements with the enemy.

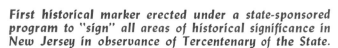
First historical marker erected under a state-sponsored program to "sign" all areas of historical significance in New Jersey in observance of Tercentenary of the State.

Chestnut Neck was the ideal base of operations. Located at the tip of the Mullica River, and on the edge of Great Bay, called then Little Egg Harbour Inlet, the Neck was a reach of dry ground at the end of a highland. Here were wharfing and minor ship repair facilities, storehouses, a tavern, and several private houses.

A privateer with a prize in tow could reach Chestnut Neck easily, deposit his capture, offer his crew a few hours' liberty, and, after taking on provisions, set sail for the high seas to continue his harassment of English shipping.

Sir Henry Clinton, at New York, soon realized that from the Crown's point of view the Neck must be destroyed. Calling two main leaders together, Henry Colins,* Commander of Naval Forces, and Captain Patrick Ferguson, in charge of Army Forces, he ordered them to *"seize, pillage, burn and destroy that place!"*

So it was that on October 5, 1778, the British Fleet appeared off Little Egg Harbour. It included a frigate, the *Zebra*,

*Name of Henry Colins has been incorrectly spelled in previous accounts, according to information from British Admiralty on June 9, 1960 in letter to Franklin Kemp of Atlantic City. The name contains only one "L." Also information furnished by National Maritime Museum, Greenwich, England to Kemp February 7, 1961.

Flagship of the British Fleet; two sloops, the *Vigilant* and the *Nautilus;* several row galleys; some transports; and a number of flat-bottom craft carried by the larger vessels. Becalmed by a lack of wind, they remained too far distant to begin their assault on Chestnut Neck until the next day.

Participating in the attack were three hundred men of the 5th Regiment, British Foot, and one hundred men of the Third Battalion New Jersey Volunteers, under Ferguson's command.

Informed of the British plan, Governor Livingston called a meeting of the New Jersey Council of Safety at three o'clock in the morning and sent express riders through the Pine Barrens to warn coastal residents of their danger.

Count Casimir Pulaski, who with his legion was in the West Jersey area, proceeded to the Little Egg Harbour scene to reinforce the local militia. (Some accounts state he was so ordered by George Washington, but this is unlikely). But the trail was long, and it was an arduous journey for marching soldiers. The force was to arrive a day late, and on the north shore of the Mullica.

Earthenwork defenses prepared months before as a result of the efforts of Elijah Clark and Richard Wescoat of the Forks were strengthened, but no cannon or other major armament had been installed. Seized stores and vessels were hurriedly taken up the Little Egg Harbour River to the Forks for safety by townsfolk, most of them relatives of the privateersmen using the Neck as a base. Three craft had put to sea before the arrival of the British, and only ten vessels, mostly prizes remained, being of too great draft to navigate the Mullica to safety.

Very early on the morning of October 6, under cover of a drifting fog, the British struck. Gunfire from the ships provided cover, and the small-arms fire echoed

Grave of Colonel Patrick Ferguson, inventor of the first breech-loading rifle, and leader of the English troops in the raid against Little Egg Harbour (Chestnut Neck), October 6, 1778. He was killed exactly two years later at Kings Mountain, South Carolina, during a similar raid, and buried there.

124

across the water. The local militia, greatly outnumbered and inadequately armed, were forced into retreat. Count Pulaski and his legion had still not put in an appearance, but word spread of their impending arrival.

Chestnut Neck, the remaining prize vessels, a tavern, and all storehouses and dwellings were raided and burned to the ground by the marauding British. Ferguson had hoped to travel up the river to Batsto and seize the iron furnace and village, not to mention the rich stores that had been taken and cached at the Forks. But the anticipated imminent arrival of Pulaski and the prospect of being bottled up inland and cut off from escape served as a deterrent, and the English forces departed.

In a report on October 9, Henry Colins notes: "... *we had in view to attempt penetrating to the Forks, ... but as the country had been long alarmed, ... we could not entertain much hopes of success, particularly, as we had intelligence the rebels had collected all their strength ... consisting of Proctor's artillery and some other regular force from Philadelphia, in addition to a large body of militia ... we, therefore, thought it most prudent to abandon that enterprise.*"

Ferguson's report states in part: "... *The seamen were employed all that evening and the next day till noon in destroying ten capital vessels, and the soldiers in demolishing the village, which was the principle resort of this nest of pirates. ...*" He concluded with a postscript: "*One soldier of the Fifth was wounded through the leg at Chestnut Neck but we have neither lost a man by the enemy nor deserting since we set out.*"

Pulaski and his men, en-route since the 5th of October to Little Egg Harbour, arrived and encamped on the old Willets' farm, south of "Middle of the Shore" (Tuckerton). There were three companies of light infantry, three troops of light horse, and a detachment of light artillery.

A wooded lane wound from Pulaski's encampment to the bay, where behind a thicket of trees, was a picket commanded by Lieutenant Colonel Baron Bose. In the distance was Big Creek, and Osborn's Island . . . and the British.

Captain Colins, aboard the *Zebra*, remained in the Little Egg Harbour Inlet area. He had been summoned to New York to assume command of the British Fleet in the place of Lord Howe, but poor winds held him landlocked. Before the Fleet was able to depart, a minor bit of fortune for the British occurred.

Gustav Juliet, a deserter, who had come to America with one of the Landgrave regiments of Hessian soldiers to fight in the Revolution for England, and had gone over to the American side, had betrayed the Continentals and returned to the British. Boarding Ferguson's vessel, he explained the situation at Pulaski's encampment.

The British acted swiftly. A ten-mile row brought two hundred and fifty troops to Osborn's Island, early in the morning of October 15. Advancing carefully over salt marsh and meadow bottom, and guided by Juliet and a local boy of some fourteen years discovered along the route, the British surrounded Colonel Bose's picket post. The boy, Thomas Osborn, was forced by the British at swordpoint to guide the invaders.

Forty-four men and Bose were massacred by the sword in a matter of moments. Only five prisoners are believed to have been taken.

Pulaski, hearing the slaughter from afar, started in pursuit, guessing what had transpired. But he was too late again, and the British escaped, with slight loss.

Again the English forces prepared to leave the channel of Little Egg Harbour. Sails were unfurled, anchors weighed, and bows pointed seaward. But while navigating to the ocean disaster struck. Treacherous shoal water and wide mud flats were the nemesis of several vessels, and especially the mighty new flagship *Zebra*. She ran aground hard and fast, and the British, after brief, frenzied, but futile efforts to free her and realizing the impossibility of the task, fired the ship, scuttling her.

Little Egg Harbour River and Inlet, called also the Mullica, scene of the battle

The *Zebra* settled on the spot, with much of her equipment, in the far reaches of Little Egg Harbour Inlet, where she remains to this day. Pulaski and his men, having discovered their massacred picket detachment, could only stand by the shore and watch the demise of the *Zebra* and the plight of the British with some satisfaction.

Captain Ferguson's report on this surprise raid states: " . . . *we numbered among their dead about, fifty, and several officers, among them, we learn, are a lieutenant-colonel, a captain and an adjutant. It being a night attack, little quarter could, of course, be given, so that there are only five prisoners; . . . Colonel Proctor, was within two miles, with a corps of artillery, two brass twelve-pounders . . . and the militia of the country . . . I thought it hazardous, with two hundred men, without artillery or support to attempt anything farther. . . ."*

A Tory historian, one Judge Jones, tells o fthe Chestnut Neck action: *"They plundered the inhabitant, burnt their houses, their churches and their barns; ruined their farms; stole their cattle, hogs, horses and sheep, and then triumphantly returned to New York."*

Washington Irving commented: *"It was a marauding expedition worthy of the times of the buccaneers."*

Thus did the Affair at Little Egg Harbour go down in history.

BATSTO GENERAL STORE
Batsto Village, New Jersey

Batsto and Bog Iron

WATERS OF THE Atsion and Batsto rivers meet at a tiny, sleepy village deep in the Pine Barrens to form the mighty Mullica River. The hamlet is quiet now; its deeply weathered cedar clapboard houses bordering a solitary main street are ghosts of Jersey's past.

The wheel of the grist mill is still. Smoke no longer pours from the vanished chimney of the colonial iron furnace. The forge pond is dry. The resounding echoes of the once busy forge hammers are mute. Stages plying the route between Cooper's Ferry and Leeds Point are but a memory.

Batsto — the village that made iron for Washington; the village that, with its neighbor the Forks, proved such a thorn in the side of the Crown that Sir Henry Clinton sent the British Fleet to "seize that place" — Batsto is but a specter of its former self.

Here were made pots and kettles, mortars and pestles, firebacks, stove plates and stoves, cannon and ball, and ironwork for sailing vessels. The Forks was the center of privateering for the Jersey coast. Prizes seized by daring seamen were brought here to be auctioned at public vendue. Their cargoes, intended for the English forces, were unloaded and transported over sandy, rugged roads to Continental Army forces at Valley Forge, Trenton, and Morristown.

Batsto and the Forks boasted such names as Colonel Elijah Clark, Colonel Richard Wescoat, Joseph Ball, Charles Read, John Cox, Samuel Richards, and countless others whose efforts for the colonial cause meant much to the success of the American Revolution.

John Hancock and Robert Morris, signers of the Declaration of Independence, were vitally concerned with the bustling

127   *The "black" cedar houses of Batsto, built during the early 19th century (pages 128-9)*

BATSTO.

An old photograph of the Ironmaster's Mansion at Batsto,
as it appeared about 1870, before remodeling

activities of Batsto and the Forks, because it was here that the privateering vessels they secretly owned were based.

When George Washington built his home at Mount Vernon, it was upon Batsto that he called, seeking its high quality iron firebacks for his mansion.

A once distinguished and capable Army general who later turned traitor to his country, began his treachery in South Jersey and Batsto. His name is Benedict Arnold.

The blackened cedar houses at Batsto cannot talk, but if they could, this would be their story. . . .

The iron furnace was built by Charles Read of Burlington, in 1766. Read was a wealthy and influential merchant and speculator, and was very active in public affairs of the day. He started in politics about 1739, when he became Clerk of Burlington, and soon thereafter, Collector of the Port of Burlington. Read later became in succession Deputy Secretary of

The Ironmaster's Mansion at Batsto, remodeled by Joseph Wharton about 1876, in the Victorian style

the Province, a member of the Assembly, member of Provincial Council, Judge of the Supreme Court, and for a brief period Chief Justice.

Batsto, called also Badston and Batstowe in some early newspaper accounts, is an Indian name for "watering or bathing place." Located as it is, at the confluence of two rivers, it was ideal for a furnace that depended heavily on water power to operate the bellows providing blast for the furnace. The swamps and streams feeding the rivers were rich in raw bog ore from which the iron would be extracted.

The New Jersey Provincial Legislature passed in early 1766, "*An Act to enable the Honourable Charles Read, Esquire to erect a Dam over Batstow Creek . . . hath proved to demonstration good Merchantable Bar-Iron may be drawn from such Ore as may be found in plenty in the Bogs and . . . in order to erect the necessary Works. . . .*" Permission was

The stone barn, with its narrow slits to provide ventilation (pages 132–3)

131

The parlor of the Richards Mansion

thereby granted to Read to operate Batsto Furnace.

Read was in partnership with Ruben Haines of Philadelphia, a brewer; John Cooper of Burlington, gentleman; Walter Franklin of New York, merchant; and John Wilson of Burlington County. He owned only one fourth of Batsto, but he was the driving force behind the endeavor.

Two years later, however, he sold out to his partners Franklin and Wilson, one eighth of a share to each, and left the Jerseys, traveling, it is believed, to the South, where he died.

John Cox became the next owner of Batsto in the early 1770's, and his manager at the works was Joseph Ball, wealthy merchant and landowner of Philadelphia. Cox continued his proprietorship of the furnace until 1779, when he turned it over to Ball.

During the years just prior to the Revolutionary War, the following advertisement appeared in the *Pennsylvania Journal* of May 8, 1776:

> *MANUFACTURED AT BATSTO FURNACE: In West-New-Jersey, and to be sold either at the works, or by the Subscriber, in Philadelphia. A Great variety of iron pots, kettles, Dutch ovens, and oval fish kettles, wither with or without covers, skillets of different sizes, being much lighter, neater and superior in quality to any imported from Great Britain —Pot ash and other large kettles, from 30 to 125 gallons; sugar mill-gudgeons, neatly rounded and polished at the ends; grating bars of different lengths, grist-mill rounds; weights of all sizes, from 7 lb to 56 lb; Fullers plates; open and close stoves of different sizes, rag-wheel irons for sawmills; pestles and mortars; sash weights, and forge hammers of the best quality. Also Batsto Pig Iron as usual, the quality of which is too well known to need any recommendation.*

> ### JOHN COX

Joseph Ball, his manager, advertised two months later, on July 1, 1776, in the *New York Gazette* and *Weekly Mercury*:

> *TEN DOLLARS REWARD. . . . "Run-Away from Batsto Furnace last Night, two Spanish Servent Men, one of them named Francis Berrara, about 30 years of age, about six Feet two Inches high, black Hair, brown Eyes, and thin Visage, takes a Quantity of Snuff, his fore Teeth remarkably wide, and has a down Look: Had on, and took with him, one blue Cloth short Coat, one light brown Duffles under Jacket, one Pair of new Oznabrigs Trowsers, Oznabrigs Shirt, a Pair of half worn Shoes, and half worn Hat with a broad Brim. The other named Francis Rodrigo. . . . Had on, and took with him . . . one Pair dove-coloured Plush Breeches, . . . one Pair half-worn Shoes, and an old Hat.*

> *Whoever takes up the above Runaways, and secures them in any Gaol, so that their Master, Mr. John Cox, of Burlington may have them again, or deliver them at Batsto Furnace, shall receive the above Reward, and reasonable Charges.*

> ### JOSEPH BALL

> *N.B. This is the second Time Berrara has run away. Batsto Furnace is at the Forks of Little-Egg Harbour.*

These two advertisements reflect much of Batsto history—the products of the industry, and the problems with the labor force, in this case slaves. Batsto, however, did employ most of its labor force, as shown in this ad, which appeared in the *Pennsylvania Evening Post* of November 14, 1776.

> ### Philad.

> *Wood Cutters wanted at Batsto Furnace, at the Fork of Little Egg-harbour, in West New-Jersey, where sober industrious men may make great wages, by cutting pine wood at two shillings and sixpence per cord, which will be given by the manager of the works, or the owner in Philadelphia.*

> *N.B. Wanted also on freight, a number of shallops to go round to Egg-harbour for iron.*

Joseph Ball was the nephew of Colonel William Richards, and became associated with him at the ironworks in the early 1770's. Members of the Richards family had taken up residence in Batsto about this time.

William Richards, according to his private diary, left Batsto on August 13, 1776, to serve in the Revolutionary War. He was with General George Washington during the bitter winter of 1777 at Valley Forge, and the two became close friends.

Because of its capacity, the high quality of its iron products, and possibly Richards' friendship with the Commander in Chief of the Army, Batsto became one of the principal suppliers of cannon, ball, camp kettles, and scores of other articles vital to an army's success in warfare. Communications turned over to the Library of Congress by England in recent years mention the cannon being made at Batsto during the Revolution.

So important was Batsto to the Continental cause, that on June 5, 1777, Colonel Cox was given a military exemption for his ironworkers. He was also authorized to set up a company of fifty men and two lieutenants, with himself as captain. This force was to be free of military duty except in case of invasion.

John Cox, during his ownership of Batsto, was vitally concerned with the actions of the privateers and the British vessels around Little Egg Harbour Inlet. A letter sent by Cox to Charles Pettit, who became an owner of Batsto in 1784, is noted in *Early Forges and Furnaces of New Jersey* by Charles Boyer:

Batsto Friday Eve June 13th (1777)

My dear Friend

> *As the bearer waits I have only Time to inform you that a few Days ago a Brig appeared off little Egg harbour Inlet & decoyed of Joseph Sowey & two other of his Boys and that yesterday afternoon a Brig of 16 a Sloop of 12 and a Schooner of 8 & a Pilot Boat of 6 guns were Piloted over the Bar & are now at the Fox burroughs & in possession of a Brig in which I am concerned just ready for Sea & a very fine Vessel belonging to Washington. . . . I think it highly necessary they (The Governor & Council of Safety) should know the situation we are in. I shall go down to Chestnut Neck tomorrow with a number of Men in order to Erect a small Fortification of 8 or 10 Guns to prevent them if possible from penetrating the County*

> *I am in haste*
> > *Esteemed & Most Hb Svt.   John Cox*

Following this letter a communication dated July 1, 1777, and signed by John Cox, Elijah Clark, and Richard Wescott (of the Forks), was presented to the Council of Safety, petitioning them to fortify Little Egg Harbour Inlet, to discourage predatory moves by the English warships. The Council of Safety felt this to be outside their jurisdiction, and referred the problem to the Legislature. They, in turn, during September of 1777 authorized an appropriation of 430 pounds, 1 shilling, 3 pence for the erection and equipping of a "fort at Fox Barrows" on Chestnut Neck, and appointed Clark and Wescott to oversee the work.

Thirteen months later, the British attacked Chestnut Neck, with orders to "pillage, burn and destroy the place." A report by Captain Patrick Ferguson to his superior, General Sir Henry Clinton mentions that they encountered breastworks, but no guns had been mounted, thus affording little protection for the Continental defenders.

Had these guns been placed, as they should have been, the "Affair at Chestnut Neck" might have had a far different outcome. Why they were not in place is not known. Cox's men were mobilized to defend Batsto, anticipating that the British would attack the furnace village after subduing Chestnut Neck, but this was not the case.

In 1784 William Richards had returned to Batsto, enjoying the rank of Colonel. He became owner of the iron works, and rebuilt the facilities, making many additions and im-

Margaret Wood Richards   Colonel William Richards   Jesse Richards

Bog-iron stove faceplate cast at Batsto Furnace

A Franklin-type stove cast at Batsto Furnace

A glass hat, fashioned at Batsto glassworks

The "Batsto Cypher," a cast made during, or soon after, the Revolution for George Washington, bearing his initials, and representing his coat of arms. It was this cypher that was used in the making of four firebacks for Washington's home at Mount Vernon. Two firebacks are still there.
COURTESY: New Jersey Historical Society

A forge anvil, possibly once used at Stafford Forge, now at Batsto

139

provements. He built a mansion there that ultimately boasted thirty-six rooms, and according to early historians lived in "baronial splendor," entertaining lavishly. And Batsto Furnace flourished, enjoying what was possibly its greatest period of prosperity.

Colonel William Richards' son Samuel became owner of the Atsion and Weymouth iron-works, and with his brother Jesse, of Washington Furnace in Monmouth County. The Richards interests represented an iron-producing empire of no mean size for the era.

The needs of the workers at Batsto were well handled. Elijah Clark had built a church at the Forks. A grist mill and a saw mill had long been in operation, and a village store was established, handling all the necessary staples of life for the workers, including salt, which was a vital commodity in colonial America, especially during the Revolution. It was important not so much for the flavoring of food but for its preservation. Saltworks had been established at many points along the coast, and the salt was obtained by evaporating sea water in large pans over fires. Many of these pans were produced at Batsto.

Years passed and the operation of Batsto continued. America had emerged the victor in the fight for independence, and a new nation was in the throes of growing up.

Unlike many furnaces elsewhere in the Jerseys, Batsto Furnace used slave labor in only a very minor way. Its proprietor, William, was a friend and counselor to his men, as well as their boss. When a lawyer, doctor, or minister was needed, an appeal was made to the "Big House" and the problem taken care of. The village store enjoyed only modest profits.

William Richards continued to run the business until 1807, when its management was turned over to his son Jesse. William then retired to Mount Holly, where he died in 1823. During the War of 1812, Jesse Richards was given several contracts to supply cannon ball, and these contracts were fulfilled. In 1824 Jesse and his nephew Thomas S. Richards became owners of Batsto.

Jesse continued the operation with the same attitudes as his father. Although an Episcopalian he built a church for his Catholic employees at the Forks and in many ways aided the employees at the furnace with their personal problems. He rebuilt the furnace in 1829, but by 1835 the operation was beginning to decline.

Fireplace and mantle in the Mansion parlor

Shallow-draft shallop or "Durham" boat, used to transport bog ore from swamp to furnace, found in bottom of Batsto Lake

The discovery of coal in the mountains of Pennsylvania meant ease of operation for furnaces in that state, and cheaper production. Jersey's furnaces had enjoyed their day, and their future was dimming.

In an effort to offset this increasing depression, Jesse Richards started other industries—a glassworks and a paper mill, operating them successfully until his death in 1854. His son Thomas H., assumed charge of the industries, but was more interested in politics and public life than business. A financial depression had taken hold of the country, and the operations proved unprofitable. The demands of creditors increased, and one after another, tracts of land were sold or mortgaged until this means of financing was exhausted.

In 1848 Batsto Furnace was shut down, the fires extinguished for the last time. Workers moved away seeking employment elsewhere, and the scores of buildings started on the road to decay.

Batsto, the iron village that had helped shape America, was fading into yesteryear. In 1879 a fierce forest fire cut through the village, destroying many of the workers' houses, and leaving fewer than two dozen, which remain to this day.

The village street today offers a nostalgic walk through the past, the black cedar houses but litle changed from their appearance a century and a half ago. But the history made at Batsto should never disappear . . . the village meant too much to early America.

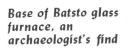

Base of Batsto glass furnace, an archaeologist's find

141

The Old Saw Mill at Batsto

The Spy House, where a Tory is alleged to have observed the production at the Furnace, relaying the information to the British

This has been the story of Atlantic County, New Jersey, a part of Gloucester County until 1837, and of the colonial iron village of Batsto, its neighbor along the northwestern edge of the county. The sites, events, and structures described throughout these pages in photographs and narrative text are a part of our American tradition and heritage. Many of them are being preserved and restored, and it is vital indeed that this be accomplished as completely, accurately, and swiftly as possible, lest they be lost to future generations. Much still remains, to be appreciated by all of us.

The Atlantic County Historical Society and the author trust that you have enjoyed his presentation of "Americana at your—our—doorstep."

New Jersey's Tercentenary Year, 1964, should awaken in all of us an awareness of our historical heritage—and the preservation of it is now up to all of us.

1664   1964
1837

BIBLIOGRAPHY

Maps
Faden, William, *Province of New Jersey.* 1777.
Gordon, T. C., *New Jersey.* 1834.
Lewis, Samuel. *New Jersey.* 1795.

Books
Atlantic County Historical Society. *Annual Yearbooks.* 1945 to present.
Barber and Howe. *Historical Collections.* Newark, N. J., 1844.
Boyer, Charles S. *Early Forges & Furnaces of New Jersey.* Philadelphia, 1931.
   Inns and Taverns of West Jersey. Camden, 1963.
Brinton, Charles. *Lenape and Their Legends.* Philadelphia, 1885.
Gordon, Thomas F. *History and Gazetteer of New Jersey.* Trenton, 1834.
Hall, John. *Daily Union History of Atlantic City & County.* Atlantic City, 1900.
Heston, Alfred M. *Annals of Eyren Haven.* Camden, 1904.
Leaming & Spicer. *Grants, Concessions & Orignal Constitution of New Jersey.* Philadelphia, 1758.
National Park Service. *Historic American Buildings Survey Catalogues.* Washington, 1933 to present.
Nevill, Samuel. *Laws of New Jersey.* Philadelphia, 1752.
New Jersey Archives. Series One and Two.
Smith, Samuel. *History of New Jersey.* Burlington, 1765.
Stewart, Frank. *Notes on Old Gloucester County,* 3 vols. Philadelphia, 1917, 34, 37.
Stryker, William. *Officers & Men of New Jersey in the Revolutionary War.* Trenton, 1872.
Woolman and Rose. *Atlas of the Jersey Coast.* Philadelphia, 1878.

Recommended Reading and Reference
Beck, Henry C. *Jersey Genesis, Story of the Mullica River.* Rutgers Press, 1945.
   Forgotten Towns of Southern New Jersey. Dutton Press, 1936.
   More Forgotten Towns of Southern New Jersey. Dutton Press, 1937.
Cawley, James & Margaret. *Exploring the Little Rivers of New Jersey.* Princeton Press, 1942.
Cunningham, John. *This Is New Jersey.* Rutgers Press, 1953.
Pierce, Arthur. *Iron In The Pines.* Rutgers Press, 1957.
   Smuggler's Woods. Rutgers Press, 1960.

SOURCES

Original Books of the Court of Common Pleas of Gloucester County
Gloucester County Deeds: Bk MM: 283-7; NJA: 36:155, 156/ Bk.W.p.583/ Bk.P.49, 50, 58; Bk.PP:374; Bk.TT: 176-178/ R:334/ Bk.C-3:277;/Bk.QQ, p.312-314; F:172,173, I:95, BB283, P:202/ DD:304, PP:99; 100; JJ:251, 252/ W:409, 610; DD:150, S:128/Bk. F.202/
Original Books of Ratables, Trenton
Memorial Tribute to Late John Richards—1885
Atlantic County Deeds, Bk. F:363/ E:45/
Steelman Family records; records from Steelman Family private burying ground
Court Record Bk. 13: 363
Record of Micajah Smith Family; deeds and papers owned by Mrs. Harriet Sander
Genealogical Records of the Higbee Family
Records of Quarterly Sessions of Court of Common Pleas of Gloucester County
Genealogical Records of the Adrial Clark Family
Gloucester County Marriages, Bk. M305
Gloucester County Road Return Book for 1810, 1811
Genealogical Records of the Conover Family
Wescoat Family Records by William Clevenger
Original Books of Ratables for Gloucester County
Diary of Rev. Richard Sneath
Town Book of Egg Harbor Township, 1794—1832
Leeds Family Genealogy and family papers
Genealogy of the Lake Family
Records of Old Christ Church, Philadelphia
Vital Records of Atlantic County
Records from an original book of Galloway Twp. meetings

INDEX